THE RULES OF ENGAGEMENT
for Public Speaking

How to Get People to Pay Attention to You

The Rules of Engagement
for Public Speaking

How to Get People to Pay Attention to You

Marc Williams

Printed in the United States of America

Published by MarcWilliamsSpeaks

www.MarcWilliamsSpeaks.com

ISBN: 978-0-9903802-2-1

Library of Congress

Cover Design by Elizabeth Van Itallie

Logo Design by John Glozek

CONTENTS

Acknowledgements

My mother was not very talkative, but her love spoke loudly to me, spoke emphatically to me, spoke wisely to me. I dedicate this book to my mother and to the many others who modeled for me what I intend to share with you. Growing up, I was drawn in to listen to my cousins Teresa and Tyesha, my aunts Grace, Dottie, and Niameh, my teachers Mrs. McIntyre, Mr. Trout, Ms. Palmieri, Professor Green, and countless public figures like Dr. Martin Luther King Jr. Later in life, I've been drawn in to listen to the likes of my mentor and friend Cathey Armillas, professional speakers turned acquaintances like Darren Lacroix and Mark Brown, friends from the front of the room like Mario Lewis, Brian Robinson, and Kinja Dixon, and countless public figures like Barack Obama. They drew me in not only because of their gift of gab, but also because of their desire to see others prosper and achieve. They are model people, model leaders, and especially, model speakers. I want to thank them all for the many ways they have influenced the design and development of my personal and professional aspirations. They inspire me. In their honor; with special attention to my mother's spirit that continues to drive me; with extreme gratitude to my great friend John Glozek (who has pushed me beyond my limitations because he believes in me); with the continued support of Sonia Laudi (who has given so much of her time to proofread my words); with the spirit of brotherhood of my closest friends Scott, Lou, Angel, William, Chris, Dean, Dan, Orlando, John, Phil, and Edisson; and with the love, support, laughter, joy, and happiness that my wife (Lauren) and my children (Jordan, Sydney, and Dylan) bring to me each day, I hope to inspire you too!

Part One: The Motivation
Chapter 1:
Make It a Goal to Have Fun

The date was July 26, 2016 when the former President of the United States spoke to me. It was the night of a national convention when he described that what he was doing at the time...was fun. I had never heard anyone used the word "fun" to describe **it**. Frightening, maybe. Uncomfortable, definitely. Anything but fun, absolutely. And yet, **it**'s something we all have to do, every single day. So if we could find a way to have fun while we do **it**...then imagine the possibilities...

It has been said time and time again that **speaking in front of a group of people** is the second greatest fear among people...second to death. Now that must clearly be an exaggeration, right? It can't be that bad, can it? After all, even though we weren't born doing it, it is something we all do. Think about how much we celebrate the first word of a child. Everyone wanted to be there to hear you speak for the first time. And if they weren't there, they couldn't wait to be there for the words that followed. You had a captive audience. And then you grew up, but you never stopped talking. You are still talking in front of people, even when you don't want to do it. And believe it or not, they are listening to you.

Talking in front of other people...it's just something we all do.

Now you may not deliver formal speeches or business presentations regularly, but I am certain that you spend quite a bit of your time talking. And whether it be at the dinner table, in the boardroom, on the phone, or from the front of the room, when you can find a way to make speaking fun, especially in front of a lot of other people, then you will not only become so much better at it, but also you will become so much more successful in life in general, because of it.

I know that now, but it wasn't always fun for me.

I remember standing before the class to share a short story that I had written for homework. Yes, she not only made us write a story, but she expected us to tell it to the other seven year-olds sitting in rows of judging eyes. I had to be ready to share or be prepared to face the consequences. I had even dared to include a joke, and if it bombed, I might have climbed underneath a rock. I was sweating; my mouth was dry. I was seeing things before my eyes...the laughing, the pointing, the yawning, the rolling of their eyes, the sucking of their teeth. I dropped my head into the hole of my folded arms that laid anchored on top of the desk. I winced my face in an attempt to convince the teacher that I wasn't feeling well.

If only my thoughts could have spoken out loud, they would have pleaded: "Please. I'm begging you. Don't make me do it. Don't make me go up there and speak in front of all these other kids. I'll never be able to face them."

She called my name. I closed my eyes and prayed. Three minutes later after several chuckles at my joke, I sat back in my seat in a sigh of relief. "It wasn't so painful after all."

Now I don't know how much fun I'd say it was, but when I look back on that moment, I realize that it was the beginning of something that I would grow to love doing. And more importantly, I would grow to love helping other people, like you, to do it too.

If you are thinking about how you can express yourself with more confidence, comfort, and skill so that you can increase your influence and make a memorable impression on other people, I would like to help you. And I want to help you have fun while you do it like the many people I have worked with who have made great strides.

Alex was a tenth grade student who desperately wanted to deliver a TED Talk but could not bare the thought of standing before a crowd to share his ideas; he was haunted by the memories of being teased as a newly arrived immigrant child for having a slightly heavy accent. During our initial conversation, he had not yet made that connection between his fears and his early childhood experience. Once we unveiled and disempowered that memory, we then worked on crafting his talk. Afterwards, he curated a TEDx event at his school and delivered a talk himself in a way he never thought he could.

Jason was a senior who recognized that presenting a workshop at a student leadership conference would not only be a highlight on his college application, but more importantly, a victory for a child who struggled with a stutter. He took the stage and spoke victoriously.

David was an aspiring entrepreneur who felt like he would never make it because of the criticisms he received about his mannerisms, until we worked on channeling his mannerisms into a strategically genuine and dramatic expression of his exciting new business ideas.

Daniel is a sales rep who wanted to improve his pitches, more specifically his tonality, storytelling, and speaking with enthusiasm to maximize audience engagement. After working together, he now speaks with emotion, uses his body language to make his pitches more dramatic, and varies his tonality to re-engage his audiences. As a result of his drive to learn and his willingness to try these rules of engagement, he became the number one producer in his company, attracting more opportunities from clients, closing more deals, and generating more revenue.

I enjoy helping people and seeing their transformation. I especially enjoy watching that happen in my own home. My oldest son Jordan is breaking through a shell and showing that he has the potential to explode into something extraordinary, especially with that extra edge that the mastery of speaking in front of others creates. My daughter Sydney is no fan of speaking in public. I tell my little CEO (that's my nickname for her) every chance I get that she has a powerful voice and a powerful future. Even though she isn't comfortable yet to unleash her transformational power through speaking in front of others, I see her potential. My youngest son Dylan is so incredibly creative and expressive when he draws and interacts with his siblings and his friends. I have visions of how he will increase the influential potential of his imagination with the transformational delivery of his words. I believe that my children can conquer anything in this world when they can express themselves with confidence, enthusiasm, and skill.

I believe the same thing about you. And I want to help you to accomplish your monumental goals. I'm inspired by this gift that we have...this gift to talk, and I'd like to see everyone transform this gift into a tool that then becomes an asset. In its purest form, our gift of gab has built and shaped the world around us. Those who have refined it have shown us how much further we can take this world and everyone in it when we can finetune the way we present ourselves and our ideas.

One day later, after the former President of the United States Bill Clinton spoke to me through my television set, it was Barack Obama who did something from the stage that was pure magic: the way he spoke; the way he talked; the way he performed. Performed...that's the magic word.

After he was done, two words were used to describe his magic: rhetoric and performance. I've often referred to the Rules of E.N.G.A.G.E.M.E.N.T. as the essential blend of content and delivery, but now I am inspired to see something more: the Rules of E.N.G.A.G.E.M.E.N.T. is an essential blend of content, rhetoric, delivery, and performance. Oh and by the way, First Lady Michelle Obama delivered a performance of content and rhetoric as well. It was magnificent.

By the way, many have said that there are certain people who just have a natural born talent for speaking in front of others. And yes, there is some truth to that...they were probably born with a talent. Maybe we cannot all perform to their level, but we can learn from them...we can learn from the way they speak. Then we can apply those lessons to the way we get our message across so that we can use the way we speak to take ourselves and others to places never imagined.

If you want to, you can open the doors for yourself to be the kind of masterful communicator who is not only celebrated for how well you speak, but also who can experience more success because of how effectively you can speak. I would love to see that happen for you. And I would love to see you have fun while you do it.

One night at a Rules of E.N.G.A.G.E.M.E.N.T. training session, I asked a room full of people who want to become more effective and engaging communicators: Who comes to mind when you think of great speakers? Bill Clinton was just one of the many communicators to top the list. Also on that short list that I only gave them twenty seconds to compile: Michelle Obama, Donald Trump, Dr. Martin Luther King Jr., Abraham Lincoln, and John F. Kennedy, to name just a few.

Who would you add to that list?

Then I asked them what It is about the way these great speakers communicate that makes them great at what they do. These were some of the responses:

1. Convincing tone
2. Gets to the point
3. Passionate
4. Relatable
5. Congruence
6. Personalization
7. Inspirational
8. Knowledgeable
9. Hard Times (I think the person meant that what works quite often is the story of a struggle that someone endures.)
10. Choice of Words

Which traits would you add to that list?

After they compiled the list, we noted that most of the traits we admire about great communicators pertain to the way they perform and deliver their words. As I always say, "Anyone can say what you say, but not anyone can say it in a way that will get others to pay attention...until you learn how." Every time I conduct this survey at any of my public speaking trainings, the list is generally the same. With that said, the essential blend as I mentioned earlier is content, rhetoric, delivery, and performance. If you're truly convinced that you have something important to share with humanity, then you have to work on your presentation skills, just like the experts do .

Then I closed my opening with this question: Imagine if you could communicate like the speakers you admire. What would you sound like? What would you look like? How would others respond to you?

They would listen. They would pay attention. They would receive your message, retain it, and use it to create improvements in their own lives. If attention is the new currency, then improving your presentation skills will be one of the wisest investments in yourself.

So get prepared to learn the lessons that have been taught and modeled by the communicators you admire. Get ready to learn the lessons that have been taught and modeled by the people who have mastered how to draw people in and get them to listen. Get set to stand up and deliver. Get ready to learn the rules and then follow the rules...the Rules of E.N.G.A.G.E.M.E.N.T.

Who knows, you might even have some fun doing it too!

Make your list: When it comes to presenting yourself and your ideas in front of others, what are some of the things you wish you could do better?

1. _____

2. _____

3. _____

4. _____

5. _____

Chapter 2:
Cash In Your Ticket

It's a story set in Ancient Greece about a guy by the name of Androcles who was told that he was going to be fed to a man-eating lion. After he entered the Roman Colosseum, he found himself face-to-face with the beast. He looked into the lion's eyes. Then he looked up at the crowd. With a deep breath, he said to the lion, "Can I say a few words?" The lion raised his eyebrow and responded in bewilderment, "What?"

"Can I say a few words...to YOU?"

The lion, curious, responded, "Sure, say what you want to say."

Androcles looked up at the crowd again and then looked at the lion, eye-to-eye, and said, "I just want you to know...that after you eat dinner (he pointed to himself)...(then he glanced at the crowd again, guiding the lion's eyes in the same direction)...you'll be asked to say a few words to all these people."

The lion looked at Androcles. The lion looked up at the crowd. The lion looked back at Androcles: "You know what? I'm not so hungry after all." And then the big cat turned around and walked away.

And that is why stage fright is often referred to as the Androcles Effect. But I don't think the Androcles Effect should be referred to as stage fright; I think the Androcles Effect should be referred to as Stage Power...because when you have the ability to stand before a crowd and influence their thoughts, feelings, or behaviors with the way you say a few words, you will have the power to achieve more than you ever imagined. Unfortunately, there are a lot of people who are afraid to stand in front of a room and say a few words. There are a lot of people who think that they're just not good at standing before an audience to say a few words. There are people who fear that no one will want to pay attention when they speak.

I met a young lady during a talk on a college campus who confessed that when she had been asked by her classmates to become the president of a club, she chose not to run for office. She ran away from the opportunity because she knew it would involve speaking in front of others. We talked about it. She listened to the message. She understood her potential. She changed her mind and she was elected president.

Whether you're afraid to speak in public, or you just want to improve your public speaking skills, you can develop the confidence to not only step up to the front of a room and take the stage, but to step up to the front of a room and COMMAND the stage. You have something to say. And there are people who can benefit from listening to you. There's a saying that goes like this: "Talk is Cheap." But I think the saying should be: "Talk is Your Ticket."

The truth is that the difference between your ability to speak well in public, to speak effectively in public, and to speak dynamically in public is the difference between being merely successful and highly successful. **Do you want to be highly successful? What do you want your success to look like?**

When I think about being highly successful, I think back to when I was in the second grade, in Mrs. McIntyre's class (yes, the same class I was talking about before). Second grade was clearly tough, but the challenge was good for me, because Mrs. McIntyre was good for me. Now as far as I'm concerned, everyone has had a Mrs. McIntyre. She was tough; she meant business; and she pushed us further than we thought we could go. But as good as she was, Mrs. McIntyre traumatized me.

One day, Mrs. McIntyre had us sing the song "The Little Drummer Boy". If you're not familiar with the song, you'll have to look it up. I considered including a few lines of the song, but the thought of doing so makes me cringe. Oh yes, I have a problem, a deep psychological problem when it comes to that holiday carol.

I HATE the song "The Little Drummer Boy".

I CAN'T STAND the song "The Little Drummer Boy".

I once heard the opening notes on the radio while driving on the highway with my family: "Turn it off! Turn it off!! Turn it off now!!!"

Have I made it clear how much that song irks me? The trauma goes back to an experience in Mrs. McIntyre's class.

She had us sing this awful song. Being the compliant kid that I was, I didn't even consider the thought of just mouthing the words. Furthermore, I was either tone deaf or ignorant to the fact that while I can do many things, the one thing I cannot do well is sing. Unfortunately, or on second thought, fortunately for me, Mrs. McIntyre was the type of person who could tell, in a group of like 5000 people, the one person singing off key. Me.

She screamed, "Stop! I want everybody to stop singing right now!" Her "Terminator" eyes beamed up and down the rows and through the eyes of everywhere in between. Then she tapped her ear. "Somebody's singing off key." I remember the finger. It was like a dagger, pointing straight between the whites of my eyes.

"Marc...I want you to sing by yourself."

A look of terror came over my face. I looked to the kid to my left and then I looked to the kid to my right. Before I could open up my mouth, the tears started falling down my face. I was traumatized. I was so traumatized that I will never forget that day. I will never forget that day, because I now value that day.

Back then, I was so afraid to be put on the spot that I cried. But now...well if Mrs. McIntyre could see me now...she'd still say I can't sing, but she would see that I'm comfortable being put on the spot...so comfortable that during the summer of 2014, I travelled all the way to Kuala Lumpur, Malaysia to compete as one of the nine finalists in the World Championship of Public Speaking! Surprisingly, and yet sadly, I attempted to sing on stage in front of 3000 people. That wasn't such a good idea for me...but (who would have thought) I was confident enough to do it. Despite my vulnerabilities and shortcomings, I became confident enough to take center stage.

I applied what I have learned about how to draw people in and get them to pay attention. That's how far I have come.

I consider my growth to be an indication of how successful one can be at public speaking. If I can accomplish this, imagine what you can achieve.

By the way, for those who might be wondering why I still hate that song "The Little Drummer Boy" even though I've turned that painful memory into a positive perspective, all I can say is no matter what positive spin I put on the memory, some scars are just too deep. I know: it's illogical, but that's just the way it is.

Moving on, when I think about being highly successful, I think back to when I first became a classroom teacher. I used to sit at faculty meetings. I had things on my mind, things that I wanted to say, but I never opened my mouth. As a result, I lost out on a lot of opportunities. That is, until I started to speak up. That is, until I learned how to speak in a way that could get people to pay attention. The next thing I knew, I was being asked to speak at assemblies, at graduation ceremonies, at parent meetings, and at professional development sessions. I was asked to represent the school at freshman orientations and open house events. Once, I was picked to emcee a school spirit assembly that was broadcasted on live television. Talk about being nervous...bright lights, live microphones, and thousands of people watching. It was terrifying. It was electrifying. It was fun. It was an opportunity that only came because I turned a habit of shying away into a habit of speaking up. I was asked to deliver the morning announcements every day over the public announce system. I went from being a classroom teacher, to the voice of the school, to the Assistant Principal of English at one of the top high schools in the United States.

One spring, I was asked to speak at a professional development workshop. Standing before a room of highly educated school leaders, some with more years of experience than me, was intimidating.

Presenting alongside some top-notch educators, known for their research and expertise in literature, literacy skills, and pedagogy, was a little scary and incredibly humbling. We were talking about the craft of teaching grammar. I took the unconventional approach of using public speaking as a means to teach grammar, not as a list of terms, but as a toolbox for rhetoric, performance, and persuasiveness. Because of the audience and the topic, I wanted to make sure that they walked away feeling they received something of value in a manner that was memorable. So I spent a great deal of time preparing to deliver the content, the rhetoric, and the performance. I'm always my toughest critic; if you can relate to that because you are tough on yourself too, then remember that it's that standard that you have set for yourself that pushes you. And more often than not, what you can produce has the potential to be praiseworthy, if not by you, then by others.

After I sighed relief that I was done, a number of key people came up to me and asked if I wanted to become a principal. What prompted that question? It was the way that I performed. It was the way I got them to listen. A little over a year later, after delivering that same talk for school leaders at a national conference hosted by the Association for Supervision and Curriculum Development, I became a principal. I don't say that to brag; I say that to prove: how successful one can be because of public speaking.

I always knew it intuitively, but later in life it became crystal clear how critical this ability to speak in front of others is to one's success, socially, emotionally, professionally, and financially. And so, in January 2011, I began my journey as a member of Toastmasters International. I joined Toastmasters for two reasons: one, a friend of mine asked if I had ever considered speaking professionally. It had never crossed my mind. She let me borrow a DVD series she owned about the business of professional speaking. As I watched "Fast Track to Becoming a Paid Speaker: Boot Camp Series" by Margaret Pettway, I noticed that all the trainers talked about their membership to the international education program that I now affectionately refer to as a public speaking and leadership "gym". True to its mission, because of my participation, I have seen growth in my own abilities. I also joined because my beliefs are aligned with those of Anthony Fasano. Fasano is the author of the book Engineer Your Success: The 7 Key Elements to Creating an Extraordinary Engineering Career. Even though he writes about the field of engineering, what he has to say is true about every single profession and facet of life: that the one skill that should be at the top of the list is public speaking: your ability and your mastery at speaking in front of others and getting them to want to pay attention to you.

Craft your skill of speaking in front of others and you too will "cash in your ticket" for success!

Make a list: What are 10 of the most important things you would like to have or do in ten years. These are goals you can achieve by using your presence to create your prosperity.

1. _____

2. _____

3. _____

4. _____

5. _____

6. _____

7. _____

8. _____

9. _____

10. _____

Chapter 3:
Speak To Your Advantage

Once upon a time, true story, there was an organization called the Champions Edge. It consisted of a team of World Champion speakers devoted to teaching you how to achieve the upper hand when you compete for the attention of your audience, when you aim to capture and hold the attention of your listeners, and when you aspire to deliver a champion-caliber presentation. Though the degree of that edge may vary, one thing is for sure. Once you start speaking, you will have already begun to experience the advantage.

Advantage #1: Public Speaking will make you Clear, Concise, and Confident.

Clear. Leadership experts will tell you that highly effective teams are highly effective because the leaders give **clear** instructions and **clear** expectations. People pay attention to clarity. Speaking in public will push you to design a **clear** message.

Concise. We all may have a wealth of knowledge, or at least I'd like to think we do. But we don't always have a wealth of time to share that knowledge. Speaking in public will drive you to say something meaningful in a shorter amount of time and in fewer words. In this day and age especially, people pay attention more to less. Public Speaking will help you structure a **concise** message.

Confident. This is arguably the most important advantage of speaking in public because if you can do something dynamically that most people are afraid to do, then imagine how that will build your **confidence**. Leadership experts will tell you that as important as it is to have good communications skills, and as important as it is to be empowered by a leadership title, none of that means as much if you're not **confident**. People don't follow leaders who are not sure of themselves; people listen to leaders who are **confident**. Public Speaking will give you that **confidence**.

When you stand up to speak up, you are at an advantage.

Advantage #2: Public Speaking will also help you to improve your Interpersonal Skills and your Level of Expertise.

Interpersonal Skills. When you become comfortable speaking in front of a large group of people, you will become comfortable speaking to small groups and in one-on-one conversations. And because of that, you will become more engaging; you will be able to build stronger relationships and develop stronger connections with people. And when you're able to build stronger relationships and connections with people, you will be able to gain attention from and increase productivity among those people, because people work hard for people they like, because people gather around people they like, because people rally behind people they like, because people listen to people they like.

Level of Expertise. When you become responsible for sharing knowledge, you become responsible for knowing what you're talking about. Speaking in front of others forces you to read more, write more, learn more, and do more research. It forces you to become an expert in your area. People will listen to you more when they know that they can learn more from you because you know something that they don't know. Public Speaking will give you a Level of Expertise, the knowledge, and that Advantage.

When you stand up to speak up, you are at an advantage.

Advantage #3: Public Speaking will increase your visibility and your opportunities.

If you can speak dynamically, people will take notice. And when they take notice, they will start thinking of you when opportunities arise. Earlier, I spoke of the prowess of Barack Obama as a speaker; he'll go down in history as one of the best orators of all time, but that wasn't always the case. I read about a political campaign manager who allegedly went on record and said, "Listen, I don't mind working with this guy. He's very hardworking. He's very detail oriented. But this guy...Barack Obama...is a boring speaker."

In the article "Obama's 'Overnight Success In 2004 Was A Year In The Making", John Sepulvado wrote about the earlier concerns about putting Mr. Obama up at the podium before he made history in 2004. *"'He really just wasn't a dynamic speaker,' says Ted McClelland, a reporter who covered Obama's early career for the Chicago Reader. 'Stilted. Professorial. He almost sucked the life out of the room.' Kevin Lampe agrees, and adds Obama's body movements during his speeches were stilted and awkward. He was so bad that when the future president challenged Rep. Bobby Rush in 2000, Obama's advisers gave him a speech intervention. Obama would lose to Rush by 30 percent. Observers blamed his poor performance in large part on his public speaking style."*

"On the night of the [now famous] speech, Lampe thinks Obama won't embarrass himself, but he's not expecting the Senate candidate to capture the nation's attention. Lampe would end up being the closest person to Obama during the speech. And for the first four minutes or so, Lampe was worried Obama's nerves were getting to him. 'He's uncomfortable, he's shifting his weight,' Lampe says. But then he settles, and the audience stays with him. And you could just see him take all that energy from the crowd, and he was comfortable because he worked so hard, and it just all came together. He had the raw talent, but he had to develop the talent. Lampe says the crowd began to swell with energy when Obama began the 'red-state, blue-state' portion of his speech. 'He turned a corner, and still hasn't looked back,' Lampe says. Longtime political analyst Jeff Greenfield, then at CNN, would call it 'one of the really great keynote speeches of the last quarter century.' 'Obama is a rock star,' NBC's Andrea Mitchell would say. 'We've just seen the first black president,' her colleague Chris Matthews would add."

Barack Obama, the 44th President of the United States, one of the greatest speakers in modern history, used to be a boring speaker, or at least some people thought he was. Clearly, he worked on his presentation and communication skills, so much so, that by the time he stepped on stage at the 2004 Democratic National Convention, people took notice; he became visible. After he opened his mouth, people turned to their left and turned to their right in amazement. They said, "Wow! Did you just hear that guy speak? He should be the President!" The rest is history; or as I like to say, the rest is legacy.

If you want to build your legacy, become one of the first names, if not the first name, on the minds of others. That will create the opportunities you need to build your legacy. How do you accomplish that? Speak as often as you can, and when you do, speak to engage.

When you stand up to speak up, you put yourself at an advantage.

Make a list of people you know who have benefitted, made significant strides, or accomplished something major because of the way they present themselves and communicate their ideas.

1. _____
2. _____
3. _____
4. _____
5. _____

Now jot down a few ways you have already benefited from the way you have spoken, a few things you have accomplished because of the way you got your point across to someone else.

1. _____
2. _____
3. _____
4. _____
5. _____

Chapter 4:
Put Your Mouth Where the Money Is

It's time to play a little game of make-believe. Play along with me...indulge me: Allow me to reintroduce myself...My name is Marc Williams. I am the CEO of MW Enterprises. Okay, so that's not true, yet. That's my made-up company, but I'm allowed to have dreams, right? Of course! And MW Enterprises is my dream: a multi-billion dollar corporation, specializing in EVERYTHING! And you work with us. And you've just been asked to deliver a major presentation at an international conference. And you aced it. Now I'm getting calls, tweets, emails, and all kinds of communications about how amazing you are. So you walk into my office Monday morning. I invite you to sit down; I slide over to you a blank check. Then I say to you, "What do you want to get paid for delivering the most talked about, most viewed and downloadable, perfect presentation of all time?" That's right; let's talk 0's. Go ahead: Take just five seconds to think about how many zeros you would put on that check. How many would you write? Think about it. Dream big. You're worth it. Count the zeros in your mind, over, and over, and over again.

Go ahead: Write down what you are worth. $ __ __ __ __ __ __ __ __ 2

After some thought and visions of the things you want to buy for yourself and the places you'd like to travel to, you slide that check back over to me.

Without looking at the amount, I say, "Hold on. I want you to take that check back and make one change...I want you to multiply whatever you wrote down by 50%. Then add that to the total. And that's what I'm going to pay you." Why? Because of Warren Buffett. Warren Buffett, one of the most influential entrepreneurs in the world, one of the wealthiest people in the world, once said that if you want to increase your income over the course of your lifetime by 50%, then you need to work on your communication skills. More specifically, you need to improve your writing skills, and you need to improve your public speaking skills. On that note, I'd like to take a moment to talk money. There's the phrase: "Put your money where your mouth is." Well, I want to give a whole new meaning to that phrase by asking you this question: What do you think is the most amount of money a person has ever been paid for speaking in front of people? The answer is $1.5 million. Now out of the following ten people, who do you think earned that $1.5 million paycheck? Lance Armstrong. Tony Blair. Richard Branson. Bill Clinton. Al Gore. Alan Greenspan. Rudy Giuliani. Sarah Palin. Ronald Reagan. Donald Trump. The answer: Donald Trump. In the article "In Demand: Washington's Highest (and Lowest) Speaking Fees", ABCNews writer Scott Wilson reported, *The Donald earned a staggering $1.5 million per speech at The Learning Annex's 'real estate wealth expos' in 2006 and 2007," according to Forbes. "Trump appeared at 17 seminars and collected this fee for each one."* By the way, a few months after Barack Obama's presidency, the former commander-in-chief, and current commander-of-the-stage, earned a $400,000 paycheck for a speaking engagement. The top-ten list above was created before he began speaking for a fee, and even his paycheck didn't top the list...but he may top the list one day. Collectively, the speakers on the current top ten list collected 4.6 million dollars for their respective single day keynotes. That's a lot of money for getting people to pay attention and listen to you. Now I can admit this: the people on that list of the top ten highest paid public speakers in recent history got paid a lot of money partially on name recognition. However, they would not have been able to earn that kind of money for speaking for sixty minutes if they could not stand before a crowd and say a few words in a way that would engage their audiences.

Some people, though, have been known to buckle under that kind of pressure. Michael Bay is the director of the famous Transformers movies. In January 2014, Michael Bay stepped onto the stage at an event, hosted by Samsung. He was scheduled to speak about their new product, a curved TV. His words were on the teleprompter. All he had to do was read from the script. But something went wrong with the teleprompter. And then something went wrong with Michael Bay. He froze. He panicked. And then he stormed off stage in what is now the most public display of stage fright in recent history. I don't know if he ever signed up to join Toastmasters International after that or if he ever hired an executive speech coach, but hopefully he'll strongly consider it because he has something to say that others need to hear. His story is much grander than that single moment. His mission to create environments where viewers can escape reality is inspiring. Imagine how much more he can inspire others the day he steps back onto a live stage to show us how fears can be conquered and how skills can be mastered. Now even if he never does that; even if he vows to never speak on a live stage again, I'm sure he'll still be financially secure. But imagine how much he could multiply his income If he mastered this Power of Public Speaking! Imagine how much more money he could make if he became a confident and engaging public speaker.

Imagine how much more money you can make: The raise. The big pay day. The fortune. You can make a lot of money, maybe not as much as money as the people on that top ten list...then again...maybe...But whatever the amount may be, you can make a lot of money and increase your financial worth through public speaking. Jeff Paro, founder of InflenceOlogy and presentation coach, wrote, *"Look in just your industry... who are the most respected people? The most well known? The highest paid? The top 3%. I can tell you without even knowing your industry. It's the ones that are out there giving presentations and speaking."* So my advice to you is this: Put your mouth where the money is. But I would be remiss if I didn't say this: It's not just about the money.

Chapter 5:
Bring Your Message to Life

In May 2013, I had the pleasure of meeting Steven Sasson. Steven Sasson is the inventor of the digital camera. I met him at a Hall of Fame Induction Ceremony where he was being honored at his old high school (Brooklyn Technical High School) where I happened to teach at the time. At the buffet table, he asked me, "So what do you do at the school?" I replied, "I'm in charge of the English Department." He responded, "You know, I wish I would have paid more attention in English class when I was in high school because it took me a long time to learn that it doesn't matter how great your idea is if you can't communicate it effectively to an audience." The focus here is to convey a meaningful and transformational idea.

That conversation with Sasson made me wonder about the way the idea of the digital camera was delivered to the decision makers at Kodak. It is documented that Kodak did not push Sasson's digital invention because they wanted to protect the state of film and photography that they had mastered. They were clearly a tough board to crack, but I wonder if the right balance of content, rhetoric, delivery, and performance would have brought the pitch to life, shifted the perspective of the decision-makers, and quite possibly kept Kodak in the picture business.

How do you get people to hear your idea? Research shows that there are many versions of the percentage breakdown of how much people pay attention to and draw meaning from our body language, from our tone, and then from our words. Regardless of which percentage you share in a conversation, the consistent message is that your non-verbal delivery has a greater impact. But I argue that it's not a matter of which has the greater impact, the content or the delivery, the rhetoric or the performance, but rather how the strategic balance of all four components can get people to listen to your valuable idea.

Delivery breathes life into the content. Sasson said, "It doesn't matter how great your idea is if you can't communicate it to an audience." That reminds me of the words of W.B. Hafford, who was a professor at Ohio State University. In 1924, he wrote an article for the school newspaper. It was titled, "The Value of Public Speaking (to the Future Engineer)". In that article, he wrote: *Knowing one's subject is only half the game. Your method of delivery, the way you get your message across to your audience, is a much more difficult matter. Ambitious [people] especially those who hope to attain success in the world, need to understand that what you say and how you say it, will count more for your success than your own technical knowledge.*

Then he shared this metaphor that I absolutely love. He said: *Your voice is like the neck of your mental bottle [your brain]. It doesn't matter what's inside because no more will pass through than the neck of the bottle will allow.* [Imagine yourself shaking a new, unopened bottle of soda. It would not matter how much you shook it up because if you don't open the bottle cap, nothing happens.] Similarly, it doesn't matter what you have inside your brain; it doesn't matter how much you can shake things up with your ideas; if you don't open up your mouth in a way that leaves a mark, nothing happens.

Hafford said that ninety years ago. Ninety years later, Anthony Fasano expressed a similar point when he wrote, "Many professionals need to understand how important it is to be a good public speaker. Your ability to speak to 2 or 2,000 people will either make or break your career."

Content is the air that gives delivery the need to breathe. In his book, The Art of Speeches and Presentations, Phil Collins, former speechwriter for Tony Blair, wrote, *"If people were more confident of the material they had in front of them, then they might be less fearful of delivering it. [Many speakers worry about how they will perform on the podium], but they do not worry enough about writing the speech in the first place."* The staff at SlideGenius, the company that has helped enhance presentations for clients such as J.P. Morgan, Harley-Davidson, Pfizer, Verizon, and Reebok, added, *"An entertaining presentation style* *may enthrall listeners, but will achieve nothing if your content lacks concrete and valuable information." (Content or Delivery: Which Matters Most in a Presentation, September 2015). The writers at Learn Pubic Speaking Skills concludes, "Content and delivery are twin pillars. To some extent, exceptional strength in one can compensate for weaknesses in the other, so that your edifice stays up and does the job. But really they are equally important and successful [communicators] value and work on them both."*

The right balance of content and delivery; the right balance of rhetoric and performance; will help you breathe life into the room, make people want to listen to you, and bring attention to an idea you have to offer. And it is the exchange of a valuable thought that is the most important reason why we communicate. The Rules of E.N.G.A.G.E.M.E.N.T. are designed to equip you with the balance you need to convey your ideas, attract attention to those ideas, and produce the results you want from those ideas.

The Rules of E.N.G.A.G.E.M.E.N.T.

These are the top ten tips to rule the stage.

These are the top ten habits to talk your way to the top.

These are the top ten rules to get people to pay attention to you.

Part Two: The Rules
Chapter 6:
Every Eye Counts

Eye contact is essential. Eye contact is arguably THE most important Rule of ENGAGEMENT. I often say that public speaking should be less like a presentation and more like an individual conversation with each and every person in the room. Think about the most recent presentations you've sat through. How many of those speakers made direct eye contact with you? And when you spoke last, how many of the people in the room did you make direct eye contact with? And when you do make eye contact, do you tend to favour one side of the room over another?

At one of the Rules of Engagement training sessions, a participant took the eye-test. For two and a half minutes, she spoke on an impromptu topic. When she was done, I polled her audience of 45 people; they were spread out across the room. "Raise your hand if she looked directly at you while she was speaking." Primarily, the hands that were raised sat on the left side of the room. She then knew where she had to focus her attention the next time she would speak: to her left AND to her right. You don't want to leave anyone out of your sphere of attention. Remember, to get attention, you must give attention. We tend to do that (make eye contact) most naturally when we are having conversations. If you want to draw in your listeners, then transfer that habit from the table to the stage. What works in a conversation is what works in a presentation. It's one and the same...except for one minor detail...there may be many more listeners whom you don't know. So that's the key: get to know the people in the room before you speak.

Start with small talk. Meet and greet people on their way into the room. Pick up on their vibes. Connect with them. Then pick out the people you're going to make the most amount of eye contact with during your "conversation". Those are the people who will nod in response to the things that you say. Those are the people who smile back at you when you smile at them. Those are the people who have that greatest level of positive energy.

I remember attending a workshop at a Toastmasters conference, which is where I met my good friend and amazing mentor Cathey Armillas (check out her book <u>How To Rock a Ted Talk</u>). After her session, she said to me, "You know why I kept looking at you during my presentation? It's because you seemed to be so positive and energetic. I was just feeding off of your positive energy."

That's what people do. They feed off of your energy. And so much of that energy is created through your eye contact. That's why every eye counts. But you can't just look at the people who give you positive energy. You have to look at everyone, whether they are giving you positive energy, negative energy, or no energy. And I know how hard that can be, but it's necessary if you're looking for their attention.

I once had a conversation with Danny, a teacher from my former school, who said, "But I don't like to look at people who look like they're not interested." I get that, but eye contact is the primary way to engage and to re-engage people. You have to observe your audience and figure out what you may have to do differently to draw them in, not just so that they can pay attention to you, but also, and more importantly, because you have something to say that you want them to hear.

So I recommend a strategy that I call "Focus and Phrase". When you are speaking, pick someone in the audience and lock in your eyes for the length of a phrase (or for about five seconds). Then look at someone else and lock in your eyes for another phrase (for another five seconds). Then look at someone else and lock in your focus during another phrase (for about another five seconds). Keep doing that until you've looked at everyone in the room. That's what I like to call taking *eye contact inventory*. I recommend the length of a phrase or a sentence, approximately five seconds, because that is long enough to make someone feel like you're making a connection without making that person feel like you're creeping him out. After all, you don't want to make anyone feel uncomfortable, right? Hopefully not. Hopefully, you want people to feel like you're making a connection with them. Remember, getting people to listen to you is all about establishing a relationship. That's why we should take that term "eye-contact" and rename it "eye-connect" because it's all about connecting with your audience. So connect at five-second intervals, or the length of a phrase. Shift your focus to a new person at the beginning of each new phrase. Focus and Phrase.

"People who seek eye contact while speaking are regarded not only as exceptionally well-disposed by their targets, but also as more believable and earnest. Politicians 'sweep' the room with their gaze. Salesmen know to look at each member of the audience." (Adrian Furnham, Ph.D, "The Secrets of Eye Contact Revealed, Psychology Today, December 2014.)

"Eye contact produces a powerful, subconscious sense of connection that extends even to drawn or photographed eyes; a fact demonstrated by Researchers at Cornell University who manipulated the gaze of the cartoon rabbit on several Trix cereal boxes, asked a panel of adults to choose one, and discovered, as they expected, that the box most frequently chosen was the one on which the rabbit was looking directly at them, rather than away." (Carol Kinsey Goman, Fascinating Facts About Eye Contact, Forbes Magazine, August 2014.)

Every Eye Counts. Make the Connection.

Clearly, connecting is a lot easier when you are talking to one person or just a few other people. It's more difficult when talking to a very large audience. So when you're speaking in front of a large audience, break the room up into three sections. Treat each section like its own individual person. Then pick three or four people in each section and look at them. Make them feel like you're paying attention to them.

Here's the truth about human nature: we love it when people pay attention to us; we really do. But the irony of public speaking is that most people are uncomfortable with public speaking because they're uncomfortable with people paying attention to them. So I say, reverse the perception. Don't make it about them paying attention to you. Make it about you paying attention to them. If you do that, then you will see that when you lend them your eyes, then they will give you their ears. They will listen to you. They will pay attention to you.

At Toastmasters meetings, there is an Ah-Counter, someone who counts the number of fillers (the "ah's", the "um's", the "likes", the "so's") that speakers use. That's important to track, but also, the next time you speak, I want you to use an Eye-Counter. After you sit down, count the number of people you made direct eye contact with during your "conversation". After you speak again, take the same count. Keep working on and gauging your eye contact, until you make it a habit of connecting with everyone's eyes every time you speak.

When you can make eye contact with everyone, then you will connect with everyone. And when you connect with everyone, then you will make everyone feel drawn to pay attention to you.

Chapter 7:
Nothing Beats Preparation

Never memorize your presentation; instead, practice every chance you get. This rule is based on what I like to call the "Common Denominator of Success": PREPARATION. Most people underestimate preparation. They spend so much of their time working on their goals that they think that when the time comes to talk about the work they do that the words will just flow out of their mouths. Unfortunately, what tends to happen in many cases is when the time comes to talk about what they do, the words spit out like *verbal vomit*. Do you know what happens when you verbally vomit on people? You drive them away. So if you don't want to verbally vomit on people, then prepare and practice before you speak. But don't misuse your time by memorizing. Don't try to memorize, and don't try to just figure it out: going up in front of the room and winging it. Winging it never flies and memorizing never lasts. But you know what does work? Practice. If you want people to pay attention to you from beginning to end, then practice often.

Remember this: Your Performance is Only as Great as Your Preparation. So you must make your PREPARATION your PRIORITY.

The 2012 World Champion of Public Speaking is Ryan Avery. When he was asked by Toastmasters International Magazine about his quest to become the World Champion, he said that he put a question on the wall in his bedroom. The question was, "What Would Michael Phelps Do?"

What did the greatest athlete in the history of the Olympics do? Various sources have documented the following: *"Phelps trains for six hours a day, six days a week, without fail. Even if Christmas day falls on a training day, he does a full day of training. Total dedication to his training program has made him a world champion."* And it has been noted that his six-hour training sessions began at 6:30 in the morning.

Ryan Avery said, "If Michael Phelps could get up early every day and practice, then so can I." And that's what Avery did. And it worked. In August 2012, Ryan Avery became the World Champion of Public Speaking. Preparation is a great habit because it's a habit that works. To make that habit work for you, you must practice this rule: One Hour for Every Minute. That is the best way to practice: one hour for every minute of your presentation. If you have to deliver a five-to-seven minute mini-lecture for your class or a five-to-seven minute tutorial for a webinar, then practice that talk for five-to-seven hours. If you're working on that one-minute elevator pitch or that one minute response to a common interview question, then practice for one hour. If you have to present a twenty-minute business proposal or a twenty-minute TED Talk, then practice for twenty hours. Now that may sound like a long time, and it is, but first of all, let's be clear: I'm not talking about practicing for consecutive hours. I don't expect or anticipate that anyone will spend twenty consecutive hours practicing for a business presentation or a staff meeting; I don't know of anyone who can spare such a stretch of time. So I don't mean consecutive hours, but rather collective hours: a collective one-hour for every one minute of the presentation. Second, if that sounds like too much time to devote to practicing, then remember that you should be just as committed to the presentation of your work as you are committed to the success of your work.

Nothing Beats Preparation.

By the way, when you calculate one hour for every minute, regardless of the length of your presentation, it comes out to 60 practice sessions. That's why I concluded this chapter with a practice log that you can use to track your 60 "reps" to an engaging presentation.

"Repetition and rehearsal of information enhance a process called consolidation, the process by which memories are moved from temporary storage in the hippocampus (a small structure within the brain) to more permanent storage in the cortex (the outer layer of the

brain)" *(Regina Richards,* Making It Stick: Memorable Strategies to Enhance Learning, *2003).*

Now I'll be the first to note that the research does not break repetition and rehearsal down into the one-hour-for-one-minute formula. Instead, the research just reinforces the impact of repetition and rehearsal. Conclusion: the more you rehearse, the better you perform. So, I recommend 60 practice sessions for a peak performance. It works for me. And it can work for you. How many rehearsals are you willing to invest to deliver your best?

Years ago, I was in North Carolina at an education conference. I was asked to speak for just three-to-four minutes. So I went to my hotel room and I worked on that speech for three-to-four hours. But I didn't spend three-to-four hours memorizing the content. Rather, I spent three-to-four hours practicing the delivery of the content: standing up, mouthing the words, gesturing, going through the motions, and expressing the emotions.

You actually have to get up out of your seat when you practice. As my good friend Mario Lewis once said, "You have to practice the way you play." After all, when you deliver that presentation, most likely, you will not be sitting down trying to remember the words. You'll be standing center stage, giving a delivery worth listening to and looking at. This is why I always tell people: The more you go through the motions, the more you express the emotions, and the more you start to repeat the message, the more you will internalize both the delivery and the content, the performance and the rhetoric, and the more you will draw them in to pay attention to you.

Now let's get scientific: brain research and cognitive science reveal quite a bit about what is happening in our heads when we prepare to speak in front of a room. When we repeat things a lot, we tap into the part of the brain called the basal ganglia. That's the part of the brain that takes a repetitive action or repetitive language and turns it into an automatic habit. You know how you don't have to think about how to walk; you just do it; that's the basal ganglia at work. You know how you don't have to think about how to use a spoon to feed yourself; you just do it; that's the basal ganglia at work. Well if you practice one hour for every minute of your presentation, you will internalize the delivery of your message because the basal ganglia will be working for you. You will have utilized a repetitive pattern of behavior to create an internalized habit. The delivery of your content and the content itself will become so familiar that it will come out naturally; that's the basal ganglia at work.

Ann Graybiel, a leading researcher in the function of the basal ganglia at the Massachusetts Institute of Technology, reported, *"Neurotransmitters released in the striatum communicate with the learning centers in the prefrontal cortex. These neurotransmitters can encourage repeat performances of behaviors and lead to the creation of habits."*

In a 2007 article titled "Basal Ganglia Contribute to Learning, but Also Certain Disorders", Kayt Sukel wrote that the network in the basal ganglia "chunks" behaviors. *"Chunking, at its simplest, is the organization of information into specific associated groupings. Graybiel hypothesizes that the basal ganglia system helps the cortex to chunk learning into habits and routines to help the brain more quickly access stored information. She hypothesizes that these cells work in an attenuating manner by helping the brain tune out information that is not critical to the task at hand: Perhaps these neurons turn down the noise so you get this beautiful set of expert neurons that know exactly what to do. After all, when you get in the car and press the accelerator, your whole body knows what to do without thinking. It's a well-oiled procedure that effortlessly comes out of your behavioral repertoire."*

When I coach my clients, I teach them to break their presentations into chunks. Then we create a practice schedule. For each of their practice sessions, I advise them to just focus on one chunk. As they progress, I ask them to focus on a new chunk and then review the previous chunk. After they're done "chunking" their sessions, they put it all together. Preparation is not a talent; it's a technique. And nothing beats preparation.

My Public Speaking teacher in high school was Mr. Gary Trout. He used to praise me for what he believed was a talent: a photographic memory. He believed that I could just look at the words on a page and cement them in my brain. Some people have that ability. But that's not my gift. What Mr. Trout didn't know was the amount of time I spent at home, immersing myself in the visual scenery of the monologue I had to perform, repeating the staging, repeating the gestures, repeating the lines, repeating the intonations, repeating the rhythms, and in essence, synthesizing all those pieces together into one seamless delivery of verbal and non-verbal orchestration. The gift is not the memory. The gift is the discipline, the same discipline that you too can practice; and it's simply called "practicing".

Again, you cannot practice the words alone. It is crucial to practice the delivery of those words. I remember spending eight months, from January to August, practicing the speech that took me all the way to the finals of the 2014 World Championship of Public Speaking. If you were to watch the semi-finals version of that speech called "Short on Confidence", or earlier iterations of it, you would notice what my wife noticed. During the semi-finals, when I talked about the girl Monique who I raced against in the third grade, instead of saying Monique, I said Michelle. I didn't even realize that I had said the name Michelle during that performance until I watched the video days later after I had returned home to the States. But during the speech, using the wrong name didn't throw me off because the delivery of the speech, for eight months, was internalized. After I stepped off the stage, my friend Cathey said, "Marc, you were in a zone!"

You too can be in your zone. All you have to do is devote one hour for every minute. Do those 60 "reps" to create an engaging presentation.

Some have challenged this notion of repeating the motions and the language until you get it: "That IS memorization," they say. But that's not true; that's not memorization. Memorization is different than preparation. Memorization is all about just the words. Larry, a close friend of mine, once said that he used to try to memorize, but he stopped doing it because after hours of trying, he failed.

I asked him, "How do you know you failed?"

He said, "Because I could not get all the words the way I wrote them."

Therein lies the problem: memorizing is treated like an inventory of words in a very specific order. That's why memorization creates this pressure on the brain.

During one of my group sessions, a participant shared, *"I think preparation is like muscle memory, similar to learning golf or tennis. If you practice it enough, then it is ingrained. You don't even have to think about it."* That's the point.

You want to get to the point where you don't have to think about it. When you have to think about it too much, it creates a lot of stress. That stress makes many people do the following things: 1) They ask if they can start over. (By the way, never ask to start over. If you ask to start over, your talk is over.) OR 2) They look up in the air. Have you ever seen someone do that during a presentation? They're looking up in the air, like they're thinking, like they're looking for the words that aren't there. Brain research shows that it's actually a distraction to look at people's faces, especially when we're looking at people who are new to us and we have no idea what to say. That's because the brain is trying to recover that information that is lost in our thoughts while also trying to process the information on those faces; not just their expressions, but also their features. So when many people present, they tend to look away so that they're not distracted, so they can concentrate on figuring out what to say. But I say that if you don't want to be distracted, then PRACTICE.

When you PRACTICE, looking at people's faces is no longer a distraction, but rather an attraction. When you PRACTICE, you go through the motions. You become so familiar with the content AND the delivery of that content that it doesn't matter if you say something differently than planned or scripted, like saying Michelle when you should've said Monique. It doesn't matter if someone asks you a question or throws you off on a tangent, because your content and delivery are so internalized that your "performance" flows. That's because you will no longer be focused on the words; instead, you will have internalized your message and your delivery. When your rhetoric and performance are synced in, your audience will be in sync with you.

So before you deliver your next presentation, use my practice log as a template. You can go to marcwilliamsspeaks.com to print a copy of the practice log. Whether you are preparing for a business presentation, a cold call, a class report, or a toast at a wedding, the practice you put in will impact the performance you put on. Practice every chance you get.

Presentation Title: _____

Presentation Summary: _____

Presentation Date: _____ Presentation Length: _____

Practice Session #	Practice Date	Length of Practice Session	Highlights	Next Steps
1				
2				
3				

Practice. Practice. Practice.

After a particular speech competition, I was asked by the interviewer, "What is your process for practice?" I responded that I've learned to answer that question differently now than I used to in the past.

I used to describe my process as an insane routine because of my level of commitment to practicing. Then I realized how damaging that response was because it might deter people from practicing, making them think that it's way too much work or that they are not gifted enough to pull it off. Everyone can practice. It's crazy not to do so. It's unnatural not to do so.

Here's the process that works for me, that I recommend for you.

Step #1: Practice in Chunks: Break your presentation into parts and dedicate a set amount of time per chunk to practice. You'll put it all together after you've internalized each chunk. Don't move to the next chunk until you feel you have a pretty good command of the previous chunk. This step will help you remember your delivery of the whole message more accurately.

Step #2: Practice in Steps: Take a walk while practicing your talk. Even if you can't walk and chew gum at the same time, you can walk and talk at the same time. Practicing this way will help you to develop a natural conversational rhythm, like the one you use when walking while talking to friends.

Step #3: Practice for the Stage: Plot out the way you want to gesture and the way you want to move across the stage floor. People will be watching you speak. So visualize what you want them to see when you speak. Once, hours before a presentation, when I stood among the tables and chairs where the audience would sit later in the evening, an observer tapped me on the shoulder. He said, "You should go on the stage and practice." I responded, "I already did that. Now I want to visualize my presentation from the audience's perspective."

Practicing this way will help you to plan the gestures and movements that you want your audience to see, the way you want them to see you.

Step #4: Practice for the Time: Get yourself a stopwatch and a notepad. Number the page from 1 to 60. That's right: practice at least sixty times. Record how long each practice session takes and take notes of celebrations and revisions. Practicing at night, in the morning, on the way to work, while waiting for the bus, on the patio, on the line in the supermarket, anywhere and anytime will help you to internalize the message and the flow.

Practice is a process. It's a process that works. It takes commitment. If you're married to the results you want, then get married to the practice it takes to reach those outcomes. When you rehearse your content and your delivery, your listeners will be prepared to give you the attention and the results that you seek when you speak. Nothing beats preparation. The more prepared you are before you speak, the more compelled your audience will be to pay attention to you.

Chapter 8:
Get Them Hooked Quickly

Grab your audience's attention immediately...because you will only have thirty to sixty seconds at the beginning of your presentation to keep your listeners engaged through the end of your presentation.

In the first 8 seconds of his speech, 2015 Toastmasters World Champion Mohammed Qahtani didn't say a word; instead, he placed a cigarette in his mouth, motioned as if he was about to light it, peered back at his audience with the same look of bewilderment they gave him, and then simply asked, "What?" In eight seconds, he had them hooked. Interviewer Richard Feloni commented: *"Qahtani starts his speech with a sight gag, pretending to consider lighting up a cigarette before the audience's reaction convinces him not to. He transitions from this into a sober defense of the tobacco industry before saying, straight-faced, that all of the facts and figures he cited were made up. The audience then roars with laughter. 'When you get an audience laughing, you've got them on your side. However you choose to engage an audience, by getting them to laugh, cheer, gasp, or any other emotional reaction, it's important to get them on your side from the beginning,' Qahtani said."*

From an article written by the staff at SlideShare: *"You will live 7.5 minutes longer than you would have otherwise, just because you watched this talk." This was the claim that video game designer Jane McGonigal presented to the crowd during her June 2012 TED talk. As the camera panned over the members of the audience, their faces showed universal skepticism: Was this lady serious? There was something else interesting about that crowd. Despite their doubtful visages, everyone in the audience was drawn in by McGonigal's words. No one was checking their email, talking to their neighbor or looking at the camera circling in front of them; all eyes were fixated on the (potentially crazy) speaker. Great **hooks**, like McGonigal's provocative opening statement, get audiences on the edge of their seats and give them a sense of what's* coming. *They allow you to win a crowd's attention right away and give you a legitimate chance to have a lasting impact."*

On July 5, 1852, Frederick Douglass gave a speech at an event commemorating the signing of the Declaration of Independence, held at Rochester's Corinthian Hall. With four opening questions, he made a bold statement that certainly shocked many of his listeners into being hooked for the rest of the speech: *"Fellow citizens, pardon me, allow me to ask, why am I called upon to speak here today? What have I, or those I represent, to do with your national independence? Are the great principles of political freedom and of natural justice, embodied in that Declaration of Independence, extended to us? and am I, therefore, called upon to bring our humble offering to the national altar, and to confess the benefits and express devout gratitude for the blessings resulting from your independence to us?"* He had the nerve and the know-how to pose a series of questions that garnered the attention he desired to compel the crowd to listen.

Those examples demonstrate that it is during the first thirty-to-sixty seconds of your presentation when your audience is going to decide that they either don't want to listen to you or that they want to pay attention. That means that it is just as important to work on the introduction of your talk as it is to work on the body of it. And there are a lot of different strategies that you can use to "hook" your audience. Whichever strategy you use, remember this: Hook them early to keep them hooked.

Three highly effective tools that are used successfully to draw people in early are Stories, Quotes, and Questions.

Stories are great because WE LOVE STORIES!!! Brain research shows that *"What scientists have come to realize in the last few years is that narratives activate many other parts of our brains,"* (Your Brain on Fiction: The Neuroscience of Your Brain on Fiction by Annie Murphy Paul on March 17, 2012 in the New York Times.)

In a 2016 article titled "Storytelling and Brain Science: This Is Your Brain on Story", Doug Stevenson shares the following: *In his book*

Brain Rules, molecular biologist John Medina explains this phenomenon: "When the brain detects an emotionally charged event, the amygdala releases dopamine into the system. Because dopamine greatly aids memory and information processing, you could say it creates a Post It note that reads, 'Remember this.'"

In his book Mirroring People, *Marco Iacoboni asks, "Why do we give ourselves over to emotion during the carefully crafted, heartrending scenes in certain movies? Because mirror neurons in our brains re-create for us the distress we see on the screen. At last I've found a scientific explanation for what I've been teaching for the last 15 years—mirror neurons. We don't just listen to stories; we see images and feel emotions. We actually experience the story as if it's happening to us."*

So start with a story to get your listeners started...because everyone loves a good story. Even if you are doubtful that you have a story that will hold the interest of others, rest assured that you do indeed have stories in your mental library just waiting to be retold! Some of them may be your own stories. What stories from your past have you retold many times? What is one situation you witnessed today or yesterday? Some of those situations may be stories you will observe during a day at the office, while riding the bus or standing in line at the theater or bank, or as you are shopping in the mall. Try retelling them in the form of a story. As I learned from the many tales told by my friend Lou, think about the message that the story tells that makes it even worthier of being told and heard. Some of them may be stories that are shared with you by friends, co-workers, or family members. Tell your stories. And when you don't have any more stories to tell, then it's certainly okay to retell someone else's story.

Now I've often heard from people, "But I don't have any interesting stories to tell." My response is that the key to storytelling is not necessarily in what the story is, but rather in how the story is told. It's the structure and delivery of the story that makes it interesting. One of the most copied stories in the history of the world is about a teenage couple who run off with each other because their parents don't approve of their relationship. The story is common. Shakespeare made it a classic. I heard Kevin Hart tell a story about his father coming to see him compete in a spelling bee. The concept is common. The delivery was comical. You don't have to be Shakespeare nor Kevin Hart to tell a story that will hook your listeners. You just need to know three things: 1) We all have stories to tell. 2) Stories are the most captivating way to make a point, answer a question, or explain an idea. 3) There's a simple four-part formula for formulating a story.

While helping my son with his homework assignment to tell a story, I uncovered the formula. As he struggled, I asked him four questions:

1. *Who is the character?*

2. *What does the character want to do?*

3. *Why can't the character do that?*

4. *How does the character do it despite the obstacles?*

In a talk I call "Another 90,000 Words", I tell the story of a former student (the character) who wanted to do well in school (the goal), but couldn't because he lacked so much self-confidence that he considered ending his life (the conflict) until he stood at the edge of the bridge and thought about his friends and family and all the things he still wanted to do in life (the resolution).

Telling that story reminded me of a day I was on stage hosting an event at my former school. Afterwards, a student commented that I always told stories about myself. That prompted me to collect stories about others. You don't have to be the star of a story; you just need to find a way to be the best narrator of the story. And again, it doesn't have to be your story that you narrate; after all, you may not always have a personal account for every occasion.

If you don't have a story to fit the specific topic of your presentation though, then talk to other people about what you're preparing to say. Ask them if they have a story that matches your topic.

Use one of their stories. Another thing you can do is read more. There are so many stories to be discovered in books, blogs, podcasts, and Youtube videos. These stories have been told to be retold by many other storytellers, just like you. So it's okay to use someone else's story, just like it's okay to use someone else's words or quotes, as long as you get permission and give credit.

By the way, I've noticed that people love quotes. There is something about the poetic nature of quotes that people just love. When I delivered that speech in North Carolina, I started the talk with one of my favorite quotes by motivational speaker Brian Tracy: *"You can't control what happens to you. But you can control your attitude towards it. And in that, you will be mastering change rather than allowing change to master you."* I love that quote. Well, after I delivered that talk, a woman walked up to me and asked, "What was that quote? Who said that quote? Can you send me that quote?" She actually asked me to email that quote to her.

People love quotes...Don't they? Or do they? I must admit that there has been a lot of debate on this issue. On one hand, quotes work like the pillar and post of your message; they support your message; they give your message a notable testimonial, albeit an unknowing testimonial. (After all, I cannot claim that Mr. Tracy gave me his blessing nor the permission to share his words.) But of course, he and many others have crafted concise statements of wisdom that have blessed the pages of websites and calendars, and have even been printed on countless t-shirts. Decades from now, people will still repeat these monumental phrases. They carry and contribute intellectual and emotional value to your message. Use them to get your listeners hooked.

On the other hand, many of these quotes have been over-used. (After all, the word cliché has become a dirty word for a reason.) Furthermore, it has been argued that starting with a quote is like starting with someone else's message which could trump your own message. Who do you want your listener to quote after you're done delivering your message? Do you want them to quote you or Abraham

Lincoln? Did I want that woman to walk away remembering my words or Brian Tracy's words? Good question. I guess I have to continue to work on my craftsmanship so that my words become quotable, quotable enough that some ambitious person, decades or even centuries from now, will begin her presentation with a Marc Williams quote (or a quote made famous by you).

The debate will live on, and so will your ability to choose. What I offer are options. So you have the option, as a wordsmith yourself, to continue the tradition of honoring great words and keeping them alive, as you also continue the tradition of creating adages that will be passed on to and by new generations.

Should you find yourself in search of a quote to introduce and complement your message, then here's some advice.

1. Start with the source before you start with the words: Kobe Bryant once said, "Talent is what makes you a player, but hard work is what will make you a legend."
2. Follow the quote with a question that draws the connection back to the listener: So what do you need to work on more to become the legend you aim to be?
3. Search for multiple quotes, not for you to use, but rather from which to choose. Then choose one that matches your message perfectly.

Where have I found many quotes that I have used? I like to do a Google search. Then I'll type in "quotes on…" or "quotes about…" A whole bunch of websites pop up. I have found many of my favorite quotes on ThinkExist.com or QuoteGarden.com. Then I pick a quote that best fits my topic. And I have to stress how important it is to choose something that best fits your topic.

Unfortunately, some people confuse grabbing the audience's attention with using gimmicks. If you take your pants off thirty seconds into a speech, is that a gimmick? Maybe, but not in my case, because delivering a speech in my shorts connected directly with my message about the importance of being comfortable with being uncomfortable. For the longest time, I was uncomfortable being seen wearing shorts, but for the sake of sharing a message that could potentially help others who struggle with being confident enough, I spoke in front of an audience in my shorts.

What if you could set a fire on stage, would that be a gimmick? It might depend on the context, but it's probably not a good idea, considering how dangerous fire can be.

It was my freshman year at New York University. I was in Professor Green's Public Speaking class. She was talking to us about the importance of grabbing the audience's attention. One day, after that lesson, this girl walked into the class ready to deliver her speech. She pulled seven candles from her bag and then placed them on the teacher's desk, forming a semi-circle. She turned off the lights in the classroom. She struck a match and lit all seven candles. That's when we started looking for the exit signs. She climbed on top of the desk and stood in the middle of this ring of fire. Then, she looked at us, moving her eyes from one side of the room to the next.

She paused.

The room sat still in anticipation and anxiety. Then, after a long pause, she said, "...Now that I have your attention...I want to talk to you about...foods that are unhealthy to eat!"

What?!?!?!?! What was she talking about? We were all confused.

That's what a gimmick will do. It confuses people.

Yes, she grabbed our attention, but she completely destroyed her speech. To this day, I don't really remember what she came to the front of the room to talk about (I had to make up that line about the unhealthy foods); all I remember is that stunt she pulled to get us hooked. The stunt was a disaster. She missed Professor Green's point: The point is to captivate the audience; not to confuse the audience. Don't use gimmicks when there are so many strategies you can use to grab your listener's attention.

If you want to captivate an audience, you can use one of the best tools that I learned to use during my trip to Malaysia: the Question that makes a connection. Start with a question. And when you compose it, think about a question that can help your audience see how your message connects to their interests, their needs, and/or their concerns. Questions are also powerful when they raise curiosity.

In 1976, the keynote speaker at the National Democratic Convention was Barbara Charlin Jordan, an African-American woman who proclaimed *"that the American Dream need not forever be deferred." She* closed her introduction with a question: *It was one hundred and forty-four years ago that members of the Democratic Party first met in convention to select a Presidential candidate. Since that time, Democrats have continued to convene once every four years and draft a party platform and nominate a Presidential candidate. And our meeting this week is a continuation of that tradition. But there is something different about tonight. There is something special about tonight. What is different? What is special?*

In 1969, Richard Nixon addressed the silent majority by opening with the questions they wanted answers for: *Good evening, my fellow Americans. Tonight, I want to talk to you on a subject of deep concern to all Americans and to many people in all parts of the world, the war in Vietnam. I believe that one of the reasons for the deep division about Vietnam is that many Americans have lost confidence in what their Government has told them about our policy. The American people cannot and should not be asked to support a policy which involves the overriding issues of war and peace unless they know the truth about that policy. Tonight, therefore, I would like to answer some of the questions that I know are on the minds of many of you listening to me.*

- *How and why did America get involved in Vietnam in the first place?*
- *How has this administration changed the policy of the previous Administration?*
- *What has really happened in the negotiations in Paris and on the battlefront in Vietnam?*

- *What choices do we have if we are to end the war?*
- *What are the prospects for peace?*

Engaging people from the beginning is about connecting with people from the beginning. Connect through their curiosity. When people become curious about how what you are going to say will connect to their thoughts, their professional world, and/or their personal lives, they are more likely to listen. So the next time you speak, considering starting with a question that makes a connection.

Furthermore, a great lesson I learned from Darren Lacroix (2001 World Champion of Public Speaking) was this: when you ask that question...give your audience...a few seconds...to think about their answer... A lot of times, we will ask a question, and then go right into the presentation, without giving people the time to process their thoughts. Not giving your listeners the time to think and respond, even in their own mind, is like asking someone, "What are you doing for the holidays?", and then completely dismissing their response, by cutting them off. Don't cut them off; instead, count them in. When you don't give people what educators call "wait time" to process your rhetorical question, that communicates that you don't care about what the person thinks. Or it may communicate that you are too self-absorbed. If neither is the impression you want to make, then pause for a moment to let your listeners think of a response; doing so is designed to make them curious and attentive.

Later, I'll discuss the power of the pause. For now, accept this as truth: the pause has impact. In a five-to-seven minute speech, with a thirty second window, when you might be disqualified if you go seven minutes and thirty-**one** seconds, you may become very concerned about that TIME that you're giving people to think. The same may be true for a 20-minute business presentation where your audience is constantly checking the time, concerned about what other tasks they need to attend to. Are you worried about giving a client too much thinking time? Are you worried about giving your students too much wait time? It may seem like a risk, potentially losing their attention to any distractor that may have found its way into the conversation. But it is actually a calculated strategy that is worth the brief investment of time because if you give them the time to think, then the message is received; and after all, that's more important than even the time. When you give people the time to self-reflect, you give them the opportunity to connect. That will get them hooked early.

When you work on your introduction, whether you start with a story, a quote, or a question, be creative and strategic in the first thirty-to-sixty seconds of your presentation because when you hook them at the beginning, you are more likely to keep them engaged until the end.

Chapter 9:
Approach the Floor With Confidence

Always show confidence; Seize the opportunity; Seize the experience. This may seem like a difficult task: to be Confident. After all, if it were that easy, half of the world's problems would be solved and history might have been altered. There would be a planet full of people always willing to stand on a soapbox and speak their minds to whomever would listen. So I will admit that it's somewhat difficult to just be confident. But as long as you acknowledge that it is a struggle and not a given status, then your mind is ready to transform your level of comfort and preparedness to grow...or rather to build. So how do you build confidence? Well let's first talk about what confidence looks like. Then we'll talk about how to build upon that look of confidence so that not only will you look confident, but that you will also become confident.

Confidence looks like your feet planted firmly on the ground. Physiologically, that helps you to breathe better. When you breathe better, you're more relaxed; when you're more relaxed, you're more CONFIDENT. *"When you're slouched, you're inhibiting prime air flow. Sitting up straight can increase your oxygen intake by about 30 percent, according to Real Simple magazine. Good posture opens your chest cavity and allows more oxygen to enter the body and brain, contributing to [your] energy boost. Plus, more oxygen = better breathing, which is your body's natural way of keeping you relaxed." ("6 Reasons Good Posture Can Make Your Whole Day Better", Lindsay Holmes, October 2014).*

"Does the breathing pattern cause the emotion or does the emotion cause the breathing pattern? [According to a joint study carried out by staff from the University of Quebec and the University of Louvain, there is a clear and direct link between emotions and breathing patterns. The study, entitled "Respiratory Feedback in the Generation of

Emotion," indicates that emotions may be caused, at least in part, by the way we breathe. Shallow breathing often accompanies fear, however subtly that fear might be felt. Deep, full breathing often accompanies confidence, however quietly confidence might be expressed. The real key to managing our emotional states through breathwork is to become aware of how we breathe." ("*Change How You Feel: Change How You Breathe*", Catherine Dowling, May 2016). So, if you want to look confident, plant your feet firmly on the floor to breathe calmly.

Also, when you plant your feet firmly on the ground, then physically, it straightens your back, your neck, and your shoulders. Doing so gives you the perception of strength, power, and CONFIDENCE. According to social psychologist Amy Cuddy, "*certain 'power poses' don't just change how others perceive you...they immediately change your body chemistry. And these changes affect the way you do your job and interact with other people.*"

So plant your feet firmly on the ground, but do not plant your feet frozen to the ground. Stand with confidence, but don't stand like a deer in headlights. The floor is yours: all of it, or at least more than one square of it. Quite often, you will have a sufficient amount of space to move around. Use that space like you own it. I once watched the New York City Chancellor at the Department of Education deliver an address to a room full of principals. She never stepped on to the stage. At first, I thought, "That is such a mistake because she is horizontally challenged." I could barely see her over the heads in front of me. And I was sitting in the third row. But to her credit, she made it work, by not standing in one spot. As she changed positions throughout her talk, I saw a little bit of her over to the right, over to the left, and sometimes in the middle. I don't know for sure if she planned to strategically place herself in certain spaces to tell her stories or to accentuate her points, but she seemed to intentionally avoid pacing in front of us. What she did so well was share herself with the multiple sections of the audience rather than keep herself still for those who sat front and center. Furthermore, she broke that wall; she stepped away from the podium that is often a barrier between you and your audience; she stood on the floor, rather than on the stage, eliminating that mote between her and us. With that said, I feel that I must share this: there are times when stepping off the stage can work and there are times when staying on makes more sense. But the point here is less about your time on the actual stage and more about your strategic movement while you are on the proverbial stage.

Treat the floor like it's yours, and then approach it with confidence. That will compel your audience to pay attention to you.

Nights before travelling to Malaysia, I arrived home to the delight of a DVD by Darren Lacroix about stage time. It was all about methodically marking your movements to your message.

Key words: Strategic. Methodic. Marked.

How many people pace but don't even know it? What do you think that communicates? If you are not aware of what you are doing with your own body when you are in front of the room, then you are communicating a lack of control over the situation and the presentation. How much confidence can you project when you project a lack of control? How can you communicate that you are in control? Plan ahead. The more you plan ahead, the more prepared you are, the more ready you'll be, and the more confident you will become.

Furthermore, when you pace unintentionally, you may make people feel dizzy, or at least distracted. Your goal is to make them feel dazzled, not dizzy. So even if you're not planting your feet firmly, at least place your feet strategically and "Mark Your Territory" before you take the floor.

In Toastmasters, we call that floor the Speaking Area; in TED Talks, they use the Red Circle. For your talk, give yourself an area and then pick your places on the floor so that you don't pace without purpose, but rather so that you move with intent. Intent breeds Confidence. If you plan where you intend to stand, then you will stand with confidence, you will appear to approach the floor with confidence, and in turn, you will look confident.

The same is true when you make eye contact. Think about it: When we are afraid of something, we tend to look down or look away. So when the fear of speaking in front of others consumes us, we either intentionally avert our eyes or we intentionally follow this very bad tip: "If you're afraid to look at the audience, then pick something in the back of the room and just look at it. Just give the impression that you're looking at everyone in the room." But if you do that, then you're not giving the impression that you're looking at anyone in the room. You would just be giving the impression that you have an obsession with staring at some random object in the back of the room. And that will only make you LOOK crazy! Don't LOOK crazy. LOOK confident. LOOK at people. And when they look back at you, what you will see is that people want to see you do well...because how well you do affects how well they feel about the experience of listening to you. Besides, most people can understand what you're going through; so most people will empathize with you and support you. They want you to do a great job. So look at them with CONFIDENCE. And then you will look like you are CONFIDENT.

But I don't suggest that you just LOOK CONFIDENT; I also want you to BE CONFIDENT. And the best way to actually BECOME CONFIDENT is by volunteering every opportunity that you get to stand up and speak in front of others, whether it's at a business meeting, a social gathering, a Toastmasters meeting, a seminar, or a workshop. How often during the week do you have an opportunity to speak in front of other people? How many times do you take advantage of that opportunity? My challenge to you is to increase the number of times you take advantage of your opportunities to speak each week.

Constancy breeds Confidence.

Years ago, there was a young lady in my class who walked up to me on the first day of school and said, "Mr. Williams, I can't do this."

I asked, "What are you talking about?'

"This is a public speaking class, right?"

"Yes, it is."

She shook her head frantically and cried, "I can't do this."

"But you're a senior in high school. You must have given a bunch of presentations before."

"Well I've been assigned to do presentations before, but every time teachers would ask me to go to the front of the room, I would start crying. I would freak out. And they would feel bad for me. And then, they would just let me do something else."

"Listen, I understand how you feel, so I'm going to work with you."

And that's what I did. First, I picked on her every day to speak in class, but I let her sit at her desk. Gradually, as I continued to call on her every day, I made her stand by her seat when she spoke. Then eventually, I got her to stand closer to the front of the room when she spoke. And then closer. And closer. Until she was standing at the front of the room, all eyes on her. No tears. Less fear. By the end of the semester, she had transformed from this shy, timid little girl who couldn't speak in front of others into this fierce person who power-walked up to the front of the classroom one day and PASSIONATELY delivered a talk that tried to convince us that "marijuana should be legal!" She even brought in a visual aid; *thank goodness* it wasn't the real thing though; it was a prop made out of construction paper. Whew!

The lesson here is that Constancy breeds Confidence. By the end of the semester, she had built up her CONFIDENCE. If that frightened girl could do it, then anybody can do it! The strategy is constancy. The more you do this...(like a muscle: the more you exercise it-the more you do it)...the more CONFIDENT you will become. I've seen the same impact in the public speaking classes I've taken, the ones I've taught, and throughout my time as a Toastmaster. People become more comfortable than they've ever felt before because they're speaking in front of others so much more. And that has a profound and desired effect on the audience. The more CONFIDENT you come across, the more compelled they will be to pay attention to you, with CONFIDENCE.

By the way, I was once asked if it is possible to feel drawn to listen to a speaker who isn't confident, simply because the message itself is compelling. To that, I would say yes, but it may take a lot more concentration on the audience's part if, and most likely when, those nervous habits emerge while the person is speaking. As audience members, we notice the pacing, the shaking, and the averted eyes. We can see you reading from the page. We notice those signs of nervousness while also trying to pay attention to your compelling message. Some people in your audience may have that level of laser-like focus. Others may be too distracted. Therefore, building your confidence, and speaking with confidence enhances your ability to engage everyone in your audience.

I don't want to misguide you though: stage fright is a real thing that affects all of us, even the most confident speakers. I remember learning about the three levels of stage fright: audience panic, audience fear, and audience tension. Audience panic is when the person is so terrified by the experience of speaking in front of people that the person may cry, vomit, faint, or run away; that describes that young lady in my class on the first day of school. Audience fear is when the person can get through the experience of speaking in front of people, but will show signs of nervousness throughout the presentation: sweaty palms, shaky hands, swaying from side to side. Audience tension is when the person is nervous just before or just at the beginning of speaking in front of others, but after getting started, feels comfortable. Which level of stage fright best describes you? I always feel audience tension moments before I speak, especially in front of new people. Everyone feels nervous, even your favorite speakers, even the best of the best speakers. The goal is not to eliminate stage fright in order to build confidence. The goal is to progress toward audience tension, and then to become less tense. This chapter was designed to give you the steps to make that progression: so keep your feet planted firmly on the ground, make eye contact with the people in front of you, and speak as often as you can. The more you do that, the more you will be able to approach the floor with confidence.

Chapter 10:
Give Them Something To See

Give your audience something to see: *It was after I stepped off stage when she came to me and said, "You* move your hands a lot." And she was right. So I started to work on my gesturing until I was able to transition from "crazy" hands to "show" hands, hands and gestures that were moving, not frantically, but strategically. The strategy is to tell a story; to visualize your message; to paint your point. As the spoken-word artists you can be, create an image of your message for your audience to receive and remember; it all comes down to, once again, preparation. Prepare your picture. Plan your movements and your gestures and then match them to your words...because your listeners are visual creatures. We all are; we love to look at things and we love to see things. Research shows that we remember more of what we see than what we hear. And the same research shows that we remember more of what we see **and** hear than what we see **or** hear. Therefore, if you want to capture and hold the attention of the people you're speaking to and leave them with something they will envision and talk about later, then show them something.

While there are many tips on how to incorporate slides, photos, and videos, nothing works better than you. So Put Your Body Into It! Use your body to paint your point. Use your body to tell your story. Remember, people are not sitting in your audience with their eyes closed listening to you speak. They are sitting in your audience with their eyes open watching you speak. So give them something to see and they will be engaged by what you show. And the best way to put your body into it is to select your action words and your descriptive words, and then put those words into action.

One of my favorite World Champion of Public Speaking performances was delivered by 2013 champion Presiyan Vasilev. I have shown his speech to many of my students and clients. He rolled up the sleeves of his shirt; he bent down to crank the tire iron; he shook Rusty's hand. Yes, Presiyan was standing on stage in front of thousands of people, but because of his ability to use his body to recreate the scene, those thousands of people were not in an auditorium. Rather, they were in the world of his story, right there on the hill where he was "changed by a tire". He created a scene and drew us into it. And that is why, in my opinion, his presentation will be one of the most memorable talks ever. And the most important part: his picture permanently painted his point in my mind: that "it's okay to ask for help".

That reminds me of the help I accepted during my own journey to the finals. Thanks to many, I learned how to brush up on my ability to paint my point. In my "Short on Confidence" speech, I said, *"So picture it: It's field day at my school. And it's my class versus the other class in the annual school relay race. And during the third leg of the race, their kid trips our kid. And he falls to the ground and scrapes his knee. But he gets back up and he hobbles down the track and he passes me the baton. And pssssh, like lightning, I'm closing the gap to the cheers of "Go Marc Go! Go Marc Go! Go Marc Go!"*

Look at all those words and/or phrases I underlined. They mark every opportunity I took to put my words into action! They mark every moment that I chose to give the audience something to see. I pointed my finger towards the space where I imagined the other team to be so that my audience could have a visual reference; I motioned my body towards the ground, as if I were the boy who was tripped; I grabbed my "scraped knee"; I passed the baton; I posed in my lightning speed running stance, and I mimicked the zealous crowd. I used my body to show what I was sharing. I encourage you to do the same to hold the attention of your listeners. Give Your Audience Something to See.

After I competed in the finals of the 2014 International Speech Contest (with a speech titled "Want"), my fellow Toastmaster Penelope said: "You know what the difference was between your finals speech and most of your other speeches? You didn't put your body into it, and that's natural for you. You are a physical speaker."

We should all be physical speakers. That doesn't mean that you have to be an over-the-top-animated communicator with Broadway-like jazz hands. It just means that you should match your movements to your message to make your message stick. If you're telling us about the time you moonwalked or dabbed during your sister's wedding reception, then do it again when you tell the story. If you're telling us how you banged that hammer so hard that you put a giant hole in the wall, then swing your imaginary hammer when you tell the story. If you're telling us how hard you scrubbed the stain out of your new pair of Jordans, then show us your hard rub when you tell that story. Get Physical! Get Your Body Into It! Give Them Something To See!

During my coaching sessions or large group training sessions, I often give the participants a copy of the poem "Casey at the Bat" by Ernest Thayer. Then I ask them to retell the story in their own words while mimicking the motions in the narrative. Sometimes, I'll ask one participant to tell the story while another participant acts it out. Participants will take their batter's stance, rub their sneakers in the dirt, motion to the crowd in self-assurance, and take a homerun swing that turns out to be a heart-wrenching strikeout. It reminds me of the age-old game of charades: using your body to communicate without words. This is why presentation coaches have recommended that clients/students watch a video of themselves presenting with the volume on mute. Does your non-verbal dramatization match your verbal narration? It should if you want to keep your listeners engaged.

The next time you have an audience to speak to, before you do so, prepare your actions according to your action words and then watch yourself before you speak to see if your body is in-tune with your mouth. That will keep your listeners tuned in to you!

In addition to your body, you should also use your face as a tool of engagement. According to Aleix Martinez, associate professor of electrical and computer engineering at Ohio State University, the face can make 21 different emotional expressions (Park, Alice, "Human Faces Can Express at Least 21 Distinct Emotions", Time Health, March 31, 2014). That means that our facial expression toolbox is packed with emotions we can use to engage our listeners. As helpful as that is to know though, there are challenges with using our faces. They are caused by the tension that you might feel before the presentation. Sometimes we can get so nervous, so tense, that our faces squinch and squeeze. At those times, you need to stretch your face.

One hour before the fourth round of the 2014 World Championship, I was sitting at a table in the back of the conference room. A woman turned to me and said, "Don't you want to go outside and stretch your face?" That was the strangest thing I had ever heard. But it made sense. If you want to be expressive, you have to loosen up your facial tissues. My secret is listening to music before I speak and lip-syncing to it. Journalist Christy Matta wrote: *"Music can be an effective tool in reducing muscle tension and calming your mind. Nostalgic music, that is, music that calls to mind a sentimental experience or psychological comfort, can aid in creating a calm effect. Choose a piece of music that has some nostalgic component to it. Listen to the music with your full attention. As you listen, notice the different musical instruments, the lyrics (if there are any), and the tone and tempo of the music. Allow yourself to experience the warmth of the nostalgic feeling. Let your body grow heavier and more relaxed as you listen."* (3 Ways to Relax in the Face of Stress, PsychCentral, September 2012).

Music is the ultimate de-stressor and the undeniable energizer, which makes it a perfect tool for creating a relaxed and yet animated face. Before speaking, I like to imagine myself on stage being as expressive as the artist I'm listening to. So I lip-sync to it like I feel it: Mouth open, eyes circling, and cheeks stretched. My favorite artist to lip-sync to is David Lee Roth because he is so animated. That's what we should be aiming for: to be animated, again, not over-the-top, but lively enough to breathe life into your listeners!

Before a game, athletes stretch to be limber. Before a presentation, you should stretch your face to be expressive. When you speak, the goal is to have all eyes on you. That means that people are looking at your face primarily. So if they're going to watch your face, then show them a relaxed and expressive face!

Now, there are times when you might give your audiences something else to see, like a PowerPoint series of slides or a Prezi presentation. That works. After all, the whole world seems to enjoy using presentation slides. Most people can't leave home without them. Take a look at these statistics:

- There are more than **500 million** users of PowerPoint worldwide. [*BBC News, "The Problem with Powerpoint"*]
- More than **30 million** presentations are created everyday. [*BBC News, "The Problem with Powerpoint"*]
- Over **6 Million Teachers** around the world use PowerPoint for classroom lectures. [*Microsoft, "Collage: A Presentation Tool for Teachers"*]
- More than **120 million** people are using PowerPoint to create business and educational presentations worldwide. [*Powerpoint 2010 For Dummies*]
- The estimated sale of PowerPoint software is **$100million**. [*BBC News, "The Problem with Powerpoint"*]
- Average PowerPoint runs for **250 minutes**, start up to shutdown. [*BBC News, "The Problem with Powerpoint"*]
- The average PowerPoint slideshow has **40 words**. [*BBC News, "The Problem with Powerpoint"*]

As fascinating as those statistics are to me, here's what's even more interesting to me: there are companies that will spend thousands of dollars (some at a rate of $200 per hour) on multi-media presentations or will allocate the funds to staff their own presentation design departments. I read an article by Carmine Gallo in which he told this one story about a CEO he worked with who spent $20,000 on a multi-media presentation, a multi-media presentation that went wrong the minute he stepped onto the stage. His talk would have tanked had Carmine Gallo not convinced this CEO to prepare a narrative to go along with the multi-media display. After much reluctance, the CEO complied. That was such a wise decision because had he not been prepared with a story and a message to deliver, he would have been embarrassed and he would have jeopardized the future of the product he was promoting. [On the day of his presentation, the technology failed, but his narrative succeeded.] Presentation slides have become overused to say the least, but they continue to be a go-to-visual aid; they continue to be the go-to-crutch. But you can turn this crutch into a powerful tool.

One of the biggest mistakes people make when delivering presentations is they rely way too much on their visual aids. They use it as a substitute for their own presence, as a wall to hide behind. Presentations tools are valuable and they can give your audience something to see, but they can never replace you. As a matter of fact, the best compliment I ever received after some technical difficulties during a speaking engagement, was, "You don't even need the Powerpoint." They are not a visual show; they are a visual aid. Remember, you are the main attraction. But should you want to use the slides, then consider the following.

When using PowerPoint, Prezi, Keynote, etc., don't put too many words on a slide. Eric Markowitz reported in a 2011 Inc. article "5 Tips for a Great Powerpoint Presentation": *"Often, people have a tendency to overcomplicate a presentation slide with flashy images, quirky transitions, and too much text. These features are often unnecessary, and tend to make the viewer tune out. 'It becomes like wallpaper,' says Jim Confalone, the founder and creative director of ProPoint Graphics, a graphic design studio based in New York City. 'Their eyes will glaze over.' Instead, keep each slide free of clutter, using one image to sell your idea. Using bullets is a bit of a cliché, but if you must use them, never exceed one line of text per bullet."* I once watched a skilled presenter use only blank white slides with black text. It was simple. And a graphic designer I know confirmed that the contrast is known to make the words pop for audiences. Consider an all-white background and black text for your next presentation.

Speaking of text, I've seen so many people use too many words. And then what they do next is the killer. They face the screen, not the audience, and then they proceed to read. Once, I watched a presenter stand at the podium to the side of the screen where his Powerpoint slides were projected. He couldn't read the words from where he stood, so he walked away from the podium to the side of the stage, turned his body away from the audience, so they were watching his profile; then, he proceeded to read. But he still could not see the words; so he stepped off the stage, turned his back to the audience, and continued to read. Unfortunately, many people have been seen facing the screen while they speak. Have these people forgotten whom they're talking to or whom they are supposed to be talking to? And the key word here is "whom" as opposed to "what". Don't talk to the screen. Talk to the people in the room. Don't read to them. Speak to them. If it ever becomes the case that they want the information to be read to them, then you can just stop talking and send them the slide show. They can read it in the comfort of their homes or at their desks. They can read it later, if they even want to bother. They may not bother if they have to read it. But they may be engaged if they listen to it, or rather, to you.

By the way, have you ever sat in front of a computer for one of those webinars that do not show the speaker, but instead play an audio over a slide show? If so, how much do you really pay attention? How many times did you put it on mute or minimize the screen while you attempted to do something else? Listening to those webinars has the same impact as someone standing before an audience while facing the screen and reading. But you won't have that effect on your audience because you will post fewer words and speak directly to your listeners.

Yes, people like the visuals; they react to them more; they remember them more. So we should use them more. But keep this in mind when using slides:

1. Instead of stepping to the side so that you don't block the projection of your visuals, try to project the visuals to the side so that you can take center stage. Remember, you are the headliner!
2. There's a rarely used-function that can keep your listeners paying attention to you: on the keyboard, you can simultaneously press Control + W to turn the screen white or

Control + B to turn the screen black. Use those controls and take control of your spotlight. Remember, you are the feature presentation!

3. Consider the value and usefulness of each slide. What will your listener gain from looking at them that is not quite captured from your words? Think of your visual aids as visual enhancers for the learning and entertainment of your listeners. Remember, you are the main act! The slides are your supporting cast.

A visual enhancement: that's the idea. These tools were created for a reason. They are useful. Just be sure to use them to your enhancement. In the article "PowerPoint Abuse: How To Kick the Habit", Megan Hustad reported, *"Some company leaders are either stipulating no presentation decks -- period -- or limiting the number of slides allowed. A fine idea, says Warren Berger, design expert and author of Glimmer, but perhaps beside the point. The problem is not PowerPoint, or even how much time is spent preparing decks, but how it's used, Berger argues."* Use presentation slides to your enhancement.

Another useful visual aid is the handout. Handouts are great resources for cementing your message and giving something to the audience that will help them remember and share your information. But be careful with handouts. I'm sure we've all been to those meetings where the presenters distribute a handout. And then they go over every point on the handout. That's when I start thinking, "OK. You can stop talking now because everything you're saying is right here on this paper. And I don't need you to read it to me." Share the handout after the presentation.

This reminds me of a six-hour workshop I attended. Twenty-fours before the six-hour workshop, the facilitator sent us the PowerPoint presentation...all 145 slides of the PowerPoint presentation. The next day, we walked into the room only to listen to him read every single one of those 145 slides. Don't be that type of speaker. Instead, be a speaker. When you prepare a PowerPoint, Prezi, or Keynote presentation or any handouts, don't use it like a book to read when you've been booked to speak.

One way to avoid reading and overusing text is to focus on using images, photos, and videos. In a Forbes magazine article, "How To Add Powerful (And Legal) Images to your Presentation, author David Teten shares, *"What do you remember better? Pictures or words? The evidence is clear: people have better recall for images than text. Including attractive images that dramatize your speaking points will significantly increase your efficacy as a speaker. In picking images for a presentation, I think there are two main risks. The first is picking an overly obvious image. An image of people holding hands to represent teamwork falls into this category; it is trite and almost insulting. The second risk is using an image that is too creative for the audience to discern the immediate relevance to the topic at hand. As William Zinsser said in "On Writing Well" (paraphrasing), if you're reading your own work and find a gem of a phrase that sticks out of your text, save it for future reference, but delete it from your text as a distraction. My goal in presenting images is similar; the image should be clearly relevant, but still clever and unique."*

Attractive Images Increase Your Efficacy as a Speaker. As true as that is, I'll tell you what has become an even better and more memorable visual aid: the Prop. The 2014 World Champion of Public Speaking, Dananjaya Hettiarachchi, did a masterful job of using a prop. I remember standing backstage, watching him and his assistant. Yes, he had an assistant. And his assistant walked around with this bag. Everyone backstage wanted to know, "What's in the bag?" Then we found out that in the bag was a garbage can with a rose inside of it. If you've never seen the speech, I recommend you watch it on-line. It's a great speech. After all, it won the championship. It was also a Ted Talk. It began with him pulling the rose out of the garbage can. Then he compared us to roses: *Sometimes, life will pull away at our petals, break our stems, and make us feel like we should be thrown in the trash.* Fast forward to the end of the speech. He reached back into the garbage can. Then, as if he had performed a magic trick, he pulled out a new rose, and said that sometimes, we are fortunate enough to find people in our lives who "see something in us" and help us to become whole again. I remember sitting backstage, watching that speech, and thinking, "That's this year's winner." What did he do that worked, that got the entire room to listen? Several things: he made us laugh; he gave us a catchphrase that we repeated in unison to close the speech; he conveyed a message we could all relate to; and he gave us something to see.

Another example comes out of California. Youth Speaker Josh Shipp delivered a memorable talk about the importance of having one caring adult in a child's life. The message stuck. The story was heartfelt. But the moment that blew my mind was when he pulled out a jar of 936 marbles, each representing a single week, from a child's birth to a child's eighteenth birthday. He then put out two more jars with fewer marbles; one was the 16 year old jar only having 104 marbles (or rather the last 104 weeks one has left to make a difference in that child's life.) He concluded by saying that it's not the time you have left that makes the difference, but rather, it's what you do with that time that makes the difference: it was the visual representation of time, that prop, that made a difference in helping his message get viewed by over 3 million people.

Props will paint a point. Presentation slides will paint your point. Facial expressions will paint your point. Body Language will paint your point. Use any of them or a combination of the four and you will give your listeners something to see that they will remember. When you match what you say with what you show, your audience will want to watch the way you talk.

Chapter 11:
Energize The Crowd

Energy is contagious! Energy speaks volumes! I always say that speaking in front of people should be less like a presentation, and more like a performance! It should be like the ancient Greek Theater: one part education and one part entertainment. When taking the floor, you should pull those two forces together to create what I like to call ENERGY!!!! Then, you should feed that ENERGY to your listeners because here's the truth: most people don't like to go to meetings, sit through workshops, or listen to presentations. Most people don't like to be in an audience because unfortunately, most presentations aren't as engaging as they could be. This means that many people will walk into the room with low expectations. Therefore, you will have to take them on an EMOTIONAL HIGH; a VERBAL ROLLERCOASTER!!! You will have to create an EXPERIENCE for them and the best way to do that is to put your passion into your talk.

What do you like to talk about? What is your favorite subject? Is it sports? Is it fashion? Is it food? How do you incorporate your favorite subjects when you have the floor to speak? In other words, how do you personalize your message so that you have just as much, if not more, fun delivering it as your listeners enjoy receiving it? It's all about your personal touch. Admittedly, we don't always have the freedom to pick our topics, but every topic can be personalized with your comparisons, your references, your stories; your examples, etc. If you want to have fun when you speak, add your personalized tweak!

Sitting in an audience watching Denise Marek, a keynote speaker from Canada, I learned so much about how to energize a message! There she was, talking about how to deal with conflict and sharing her C.A.L.M. framework. Instead of just listing the strategies, she energized the crowd with her personal stories, like the one about jumping off and on a platform to liven up the crowd, only to break her heel and pop the buttons on her dress. She clearly enjoys telling that story. I could tell by the way she told it. That joy was contagious!

Searching through Youtube, I found a Steve Jobs' talk about marketing. I was waiting for the facts and figures and the statistics that show the biggest impact on sales and stocks. But Mr. Jobs did not suit up to suck the energy out of the room with numbers. Instead, in a sweater and shorts, he energized the room with a talk about core values and this notion that there are people in this world crazy enough to "Think Different". In that talk, he mentioned how moved he was to share his message. When you can be moved by your own message, then you can create the energy to move your audience. The feeling is contagious! And that is true even when your audience may not be interested in your topic.

Many years ago, there was a student in my class named Anthony who loved talking about his favorite topic: professional wrestling. As soon as he said those two words ("professional" and "wrestling"), I could see the eyes across the room roll back into every other kid's head. Someone yelled out, "Man, don't you know that stuff is fake?!" But that comment didn't phase Anthony because he was so excited to talk about his favorite topic. He talked about his favorite wrestlers: The Rock, John Cena, Stone Cold Steve Austin, and every other wrestling star he imagined himself to be. He would attempt to connect any topic to professional wrestling. And by the time he was done with any of his speeches...everyone in the room who wasn't interested in professional wrestling at the beginning of that speech...still wasn't interested in professional wrestling by the end of that speech. But, they couldn't stop talking about his presentation because his energy was contagious!

Your energy can be infectious too! Now some people have that natural energy! And some people need a boost! Which best describes you? How do you get pumped before you talk? Is it your personal touch that amps you up or is it your pre-talk warm-up?

In a Forbes Magazine article, Carmine Gallo shared Tony Robbins' pre-speaking ritual: incantations, affirmations, and lots of movement. *"This makes sense since one of Robbins' core teachings is that energized movement can change your state of mind. Robbins gets himself in the zone for about ten minutes prior to taking the stage. He jumps up and down, spins around, fist pumps, stands with his arms outstretched, and even bounces on a trampoline."*

You may not have a trampoline, at least not an easily accessible one that you can use before you take the floor. Neither do I, but I do have a pre-talk warm-up routine that also includes a lot of movement. It involves a lot of music. Music can change your mood. Music can lure those butterflies in your stomach and put them into formation. That's what it does for me. Music Moves Me. If it moves you too, then plug into it before you take the floor. Move your body. Move your crowd.

Step One: Three hours before your presentation, listen to your favorite music. On my way to a conference where I was scheduled to present, the rain was pouring and the vision was foggy. My eyes were squinting the road into focus. But as serious as I kept my concentration on the road, I was getting in the zone too. Through the speakers, my favorite music pumped me full of energy: It was a one-man party in that car. How often do you sing out loud in your car? That was me. I was driving safely, and at the same time, I was getting ready. Energy was on the rise! To reach that level each time, I've prepared my pre-talk playlist. I encourage you to do the same. Before you present, pick your playlist. If you don't have one, then create your list right now.

Here are some of my favorites that I have grooved to minutes before for a presentation. But my list is much more extensive than this:

Lose Your Yourself (Eminem)	Without Me (Halsey)
Welcome to My Hood (DJ Khaled)	Signs (Snoop Dogg)
Training Montage (Vince DiCola)	Forever (Drake)
Wanna Be Startin' Somethin' (MJ)	Smile (Kirk Franklin)

What would you put on your playlist?

Pre-Presentation Playlist

Before you present, pick your playlist. If you don't have one for the occasion, then create your list.

Title: _____

Artist: _____

Title: _____

Artist: _____

Title: _____

Artist: _____

Title: _____

Artist: _____

Title: _____

Artist: _____

Title: _____

Artist: _____

You can go to marcwilliamsspeaks.com to print a copy of the pre-presentation playlist.

If there were cameras in the staircase of the Convention Center in Kuala Lumpur, you would have seen me rocking out to the tunes of some old school hip-hop and some classic 80's pop hits. And during the District competition, before the contest began and after the woman had suggested that I stretch my face, I took a walk outside. I stepped to the rhythm as I circled the parking lot, around the perimeter of the hotel. My head was bopping. My hips were shaking. My legs were jamming. I was dancing in the parking lot. And every once in a while, I would stop to practice my speech. Then, I'd go back to dancing in the parking lot. One man approached me to ask if I was attending the wedding in the hotel. He was ready to invite me to the reception, but I told him I was practicing my speech. "Looks like you're going to have a lot of fun delivering that speech," he said. I replied, "That's the key: rule number one is have fun." He wished me luck and walked away in the shadows of my dancing feet.

Plug in your headphones and play your favorite music: music that boosts your energy, tunes that build your excitement, songs that change your mood, like dance music, workout music, or good times, great memories music. Music transforms the way you feel. Dance like the people in that Justin Timberlake video before you deliver your talk. In Timberlake's "Can't Stop the Feeling" video, there's a cast of people from different walks of life, dancing to one tune and having fun. Music is fun! Fun is energy! So energize your fun! Play your list and party before you present! Whether you actually start dancing, swiveling your hips, or just swaying back and forth, you should get your body moving. Tap your feet. Clap your hands. Nod your head. Move! Motion builds energy. And energy moves crowds. Your pre-talk warm-up should be like the pre-game warm-up of Lebron James, Kevin Durant, and Stephen Curry. You've probably seen them walking into the arenas with their headphones on, bopping their heads and getting into their zones. That's what you should do: Get into your zone, your pre-presentation party zone.

Step Two: Two hours before your presentation, practice it. Go through your routine and get into your flow, just like NBA legend Ray

Allen used to do. Ray Allen would go onto the court hours before the game, hours before anyone else, just to shoot the ball around, just so that he could get into his flow. That's what I want you to do: get into your presentation flow. If time does not permit you to run through the entire talk, then at least jog through your opening and your closing. After you get into your zone, get into your flow.

Step Three: One hour before the presentation, relax. Put the music back on, but relax. Keep your movements limited and relaxed. Get into that Michael Phelps' zone. Remember that image from the 2016 Summer Olympics that went viral after Phelps sat poolside with his headphones on, with the meanest scowl on his face. Nothing could distract him, not even his very energetic rival. Phelps sat still while the music coursed through his veins. He was in the Wooden Zone.

One of the greatest basketball coaches of all time is John Wooden. Coach Wooden said that no athlete should ever get too worked up right before a game. Similarly, no presenter should get too worked up right before a presentation. By the way, what an athlete goes through right before an athletic competition is similar to what people go through right before a presentation: increased heart rate, increased muscle tension, increased tension in the chest and throat, and a rush of adrenaline. It's the conditions of "flight or fight". And just like the athlete who won't flee from the opportunity to be victorious, you must not flee from the opportunity to be spectacular. Go for it! But before you get too pumped up, save that energy for game time, or in this case, save it for your stage time. Harness your energy. After you get into the zone and get into your flow, step into your state of calm. When you listen to your music this time, try not to tap your feet too much; try not to nod your head too much; try not to wiggle your hips too much. Then, right before you present, stand up and stretch your legs. Don't sit for very long right before you present. When you sit for too long, your body can become dormant. You need to exert just a little energy before you speak, so get your body moving slightly. Loosen up your body with a slight bounce and some controlled breathing.

The hardest part for me during speech contests has been picking a late number and then sitting and waiting for over an hour to speak. I was speaker # 8 in the 2014 District competition. As Speaker #7 was introduced, a friend of mine, June, said, "You should stand up now and walk around to get the blood flowing." You should do the same. Visualize it this way: You're about to take the floor and win over the crowd! The curtain is about to open. Your theme music is about to play. Your pyro is about to explode. The crowd is cheering your name. No, you are not a professional wrestler, but you are about to become a superstar! But first, be sure to warm-up. Before you talk: Build the Energy; Store the Energy, Release the Energy. When you are energetic, your audience is energized. And when your audience is energized, your audience is engaged. That's how you get them to pay attention to you.

I must add this: It was a Sunday morning when I was standing in line to check out of the hotel in Kuala Lumpur. That's when I met Vanessa from Hong Kong. She repeated a line from my finals speech. Then she said, "I liked your speech, but I still think Dananjaya should have won." I responded, "That's okay. No offense taken. He delivered a great speech."

She continued, "But there were a couple of people who said a few things about your speech that I didn't necessarily agree with, but I thought I'd share them with you. They said that you had kung-fu feet."

"I have no idea what that means."

"Well when you came on to the stage, you started like this (she mimicked a kung-fu fighting stance). And then you exploded with this energy."

Energy. That's a good thing, right? Yes, it is, however...she continued...

"It was too overwhelming at the beginning of the speech."

When you start so high at the beginning of your speech, it's hard to go higher. What you want to do is to create that rollercoaster of emotions. Rollercoasters start with a slow incline to build the anticipation. Then they drop fast for the adrenaline rush. Other than the

Aerosmith rollercoaster at Disney, all, or most other rollercoasters, to my knowledge, start with a build up, rather than an explosive start. You should begin the same way.

When I shared Vanessa's comment with my wife, she added, "I told you so." She did; she gave me the same advice weeks before I even qualified to go to Malaysia. When I was working on the "Short on Confidence" speech, my wife yelled, "Whoa! Whoa! Whoa! Calm down when you start. And then build it up."

Energy is most powerful when it is unleashed methodically. So build your energy: build it gradually and then fluctuate it strategically. When you do so, your listeners will follow.

Energy Excites. Energy Entertains. Energy Engages.

Chapter 12:
Make Your Point Clear

Make a point and make an outline; Organization is key. One of the most challenging things about speaking in public is that we may have a wealth of knowledge, but we don't always create an order by which to share that information. Imagine standing before a crowd or across from an interviewer when all of a sudden, even though you have all the right answers, you start rambling on or spitting out random thoughts. Things then get awkward because your listeners have no idea what you're trying to say. They can't follow you. And if your audience can't follow you, then your audience will stop paying attention to you.

What can you do to make sure that doesn't happen to you?

First, summarize your message in one sentence, or for my 21st Century communicators, summarize your message in one tweet (140 characters). Whether you are preparing for an interview, writing a college essay, drafting a book, composing an essay/research paper, or preparing a presentation, summarize your message in a short sentence of 10-12 words. I learned that technique from a few former Toastmaster World Champions, including Darren Lacroix, Mark Brown, and Craig Valentine. I use it all the time. I have pushed my clients and my students to use it too. I'm guilty of counting on my fingers how many words I have used to compose a message. It's a challenge that is worth the work. Whether or not you hold yourself to such a small word count, keep it brief. A concise statement of your message will give you the clarity you need to give your listeners the clarity they need.

Let's try it. Below is a draft of a talk I worked on with one of my mentors to help an audience of attention-seekers. How would you summarize the message in 10-12 words, no more, no less? And how would you summarize your message in the same concise manner?

My mother used to sing the song, "This little light of mine, I'm gonna let it shine. Let it shine. Let it shine. Let it shine." That is a beautiful song, but what do you do when you think that your light, your personality, your identity is not bright enough to shine? Do you try to do something else to stand out? I used to ask myself, "What do I have to do to get people to pay attention to me?" One day, I would learn the answer.

Pause to Ponder: To create your point, pose a question that you would like to answer. For example, "What do you have to do to get people to pay attention to you?"

But first, let me take you back to when I was growing up in Brooklyn, New York where the most popular thing for a kid to do in my neighborhood was to go up to the roof of our apartment building. One day I went up there, but it didn't feel like I had expected. So I went down to the park. Later in the day, this kid says, "Hey yo Marc, did I see you on the roof this morning?" I replied, "Yeah, you did." He said, "Well I dare you to go up there again." I said, "OK." He said, "No. Wait. I'm not finished yet." He said, "I dare you to go up there again...and jump off."

So I looked at him as if I couldn't believe what he just asked me to do. Then I said..."OK."

Pause to Ponder: To illustrate your point, add dialogue, especially that which supports your message. For example, the words of a boy that show how much he welcomed getting attention.

Next thing I knew, I was standing on the roof of this eight-story building, looking down at a crowd of people. It was like standing on stage in front of hundreds of people, competing in an International Speech contest. All eyes on me, like I wanted. But then I got scared. I turned away and walked down to my apartment. And there stood my mother. She said, "Marc, were you just on the roof?"

Pause to Ponder: To emphasize your point, use a phrase that could be repeated throughout the presentation. For example, "All eyes on me, like I wanted."

Like any kid who's ever done something he wasn't supposed to do, I said..."No."

She said, "Yeah, alright. Well listen, if anyone ever asks you to go on that roof and jump off, you tell them, 'No. I don't have to do anything crazy for attention but be myself." Wise words from a wise woman, but I didn't get it.

So then I went on to high school where I tried to do something else to stand out. But this time, I wouldn't try to fly, but as they said in the 1980's, I would try to "look fly". Have you ever seen someone who wore something just to grab attention? One morning, I was getting dressed for school and I took this t-shirt and wrapped it around my knee. And I walked around the school, looking...ridiculous. This one teacher, Mr. Baskerville, asked me, "Why do you have that shirt wrapped around your knee?"

Pause to Ponder: To build your point, tell stories. How many stories do you need to make a point? One will be suffice in most cases, but 2-3 might work, depending on the time you have and the entertainment value of the stories.

I looked at him like I was confused by the question and I said, "I don't know." He said, " Well I just want you to know that you don't have to DO anything crazy to get attention but BE yourself." Wise words from a wise man, but I didn't get it. Then I realized that because I didn't think there was anything special about me to notice, I was trying to create something special about myself and I didn't realize that you don't have to do that. I find it significant that I began to learn that when I was a student in high school because eventually I would become a teacher in the very same high school. And the most important thing that I teach our kids are the words of Dwight Moody, a 19th Century American preacher, who once said, "We are often told to let our light shine, and when it does, we don't have to tell anyone that it does." Then he said, "Lighthouses don't fire cannons to call attention to their shining. They just shine."

Pause to Ponder: To support your point, cite the words of a famous person or of someone you know. For example, "Lighthouses don't fire cannons to call attention to their shining. They just shine."

That makes me think of Rodney. Rodney was a student who was failing my class. I would encourage him to keep trying, but instead of focusing on his school work, he started acting out in school: calling out in class, starting fights, arguing with teachers. One day, he showed up to school drunk. The principal wanted him suspended, but I asked if I could talk to Rodney. When I asked him, "Why did you try to drink a whole bottle of vodka?", he said..."Because I just wanted everyone to think I was cool."

So I said to him what my mother said to me. He said, " But you don't understand Mr. Williams." I said, "I think I do." Then I invited him to meet with me once a week. At first, I tried to come up with this mind-blowing tactic that was going to change his life and make me that superstar teacher. But then I changed my mind. I just talked and listened.

Pause to Ponder: To make your point, give the credit of wisdom to someone else whenever you can and mark the moment the message was taught to you. For example, "So I told him what my mother said to me."

One day though, he said, " Mr. Williams, I'm sorry to disappoint you but I got in trouble today. But I didn't pull the fire alarm. They wanted me to do it, but I didn't do it. But I was with them."
I said, "Don't worry about it. You just keep working on yourself like I taught you."
He said, "But that hasn't worked."

So I told him that the principal stopped me the other day and said, "Marc, you know that kid you've been working with who was getting into all that trouble? I saw him the other day and he seems like a new person, like his spirit has been lifted."

I told Rodney: "See, other people have noticed that you are changing. So you're right. What I've taught you hasn't worked yet. But what I've taught you is a work in progress."

He said, "Nah Mr. Williams, you're wrong. I'm not changing. I'm just finally starting to learn to be comfortable with who I am. And you know why."
I said, "Why?"
He said, "Because you paid attention to me. So I paid attention to me too."

Pause to Ponder: To highlight your point, play with your wording. For example, "Because you paid attention to me. So I paid attention to me too."

That's when I finally got it. I didn't do anything else to help him but be myself. It's not easy being ourselves sometimes, is it?
But when we focus less on the things that don't make us superstars and more on who we naturally are, that is when we shine. And when we focus more on what we see in ourselves and less on what others see in us, because we can't control what they think of us anyway, that is when we shine.
I learned that if you want people to pay attention to you, you don't have to climb to an unnecessary height, or jump a far and dangerous distance, or try to look or be different.
If you want people to pay attention to you, all you have to do is just be you...and let your light shine.

Pause to Ponder: To clarify your point, summarize it in a concise phrase.

So how would you summarize the message of that speech? Remember, only use 10-12 words.

_____

_____

_____

I'll share my summary statement at the end of this chapter.

Let's try another one.

This is from a 2013 commencement speech delivered by Richard Branson:

The best advice I could give any graduate is to spend your time working on whatever you are passionate about in life. If your degree was focused upon one particular area, don't let that stop you from moving in another direction. If college hasn't worked out for you, don't let that put you off. Virgin's expansion into so many different areas is borne out of my insatiable curiosity to enjoy new experiences and pursue fresh challenges.

Pause to Ponder: Your message is your advice. Notice how Branson began with his best advice.

You may decide to take a break and consider your options. I would urge you to travel, take on new experiences and draw upon those when it comes to making the decisions that will shape your future. The amount of business ideas that people pick up from travelling the world is enormous. If you don't want to reinvent the wheel, you may find a business that works in another market that could be adapted for your own. Gap years don't only have to happen before you go to college. Actually, a good option is to travel instead of going to university. You can work and still have a lot of fun along the way: you won't create as much debt, you'll learn an awful lot and may come back with some great ideas.

Pause to Ponder: Your examples build upon your message. Notice how Branson offers an example of travelling to generate new ideas.

Equally, if you spot an opportunity early on and are really excited by it, throw yourself into it with everything you have got. Be ambitious.

There probably won't be another time in your life when you have such freedom of opportunity. Grasp it with both hands. If you can't find an opening that fits what you want to do, why not try to create one? We always enter markets where the leaders are not doing a great job, so we can go in and disrupt them by offering better quality services.

Until this week I had never had a boss in my entire life. I lasted about five hours before Tony Fernandes sacked me, after throwing a tray of drinks over him while working as a stewardess on a flight! (It was all for a bet to raise money for charity, so I wasn't too upset.)

Pause to Ponder: Key words emphasize your message. Notice how Branson emphasizes following your passion by using words like "fun" and "freedom".

My own transition from education to a working life was pretty straightforward.

I started Student Magazine at school and was spending an increasingly large amount of time working on getting it off the ground. The headmaster gave me an ultimatum: he said if I wanted to carry on with Student, I had to stop being a student. So I left to start my adventures in business. Being dyslexic, I never excelled in the classroom and entrepreneurship wasn't encouraged. I didn't even know what I was doing was called entrepreneurship until somebody told me!

Pause to Ponder: Personal stories make a point like no other device. Notice how Branson uses his experience and the advice from his headmaster to model his message.

However, education is absolutely crucial to success and to the progress of the world at large. As Nelson Mandela said: "Education is the most powerful weapon to change the world."

But education doesn't take place in stuffy classrooms and university buildings; it can happen everywhere, every day to every person. I was on a panel at a University in Australia recently and it turned out the only one of us onstage who had graduated was the Dean himself!

I have been offered to do graduation speeches over the years and did accept an honorary Doctor of Technology from Loughborough University. It was strange at the time, but now that we have Virgin Galactic perhaps it's not so strange! I was chuffed to receive it, having left school at 15. It was a hell of a lot easier than going through university to get it! If you are graduating, congratulations and good luck for your future. Every graduate – scratch that – every person has the chance to reach for the stars in their chosen field.

Pause to Ponder: To clarify your point, summarize it in a concise phrase, most effectively towards the end of your presentation.

Write your 10-12 word summary of Sir Richard Branson's message:

_____

_____

_____

Summarize your message in a brief statement and then include that statement in your presentation; repeat it a few times throughout the presentation to make your message stick. When your message is clearly stated, your audience will retain it.

Second, divide your message into parts, whether it be three points, a series of stories, a numerical list of tips, or an acronym.

The Rule of Thirds: The Rule of Thirds isn't just an application in photography to create the best image. It also applies to the construction of a well-developed message.

When I teach the Rules of Engagement, I discuss the personal and professional benefits of being a good public speaker; second, the financial benefits of being a good public speaker; and third, the Rules of Engagement.

In a 2012 Forbes magazine article, Carmine Gallo (communications coach and author) wrote: *"Steve Jobs applied the Rule of 3 in nearly every presentation and product launch. In 2007 Jobs introduced the first iPhone as the 'third' of Apple's revolutionary product categories (the first two were the Macintosh and the iPod). He even said that Apple would be introducing 'three' revolutionary products—a new iPod, a phone, and an Internet communications device. Jobs repeated the three products slowly until the audience finally figured out he was talking about one device capable of handling all three tasks...Try to apply the Rule of 3. Divide a presentation into three parts. Introduce a product with three benefits. Give me three reasons to hire you! The rule of 3—It worked for [Thomas] Jefferson, it worked for Jobs, and it will work for you."*

You may be able to connect this to the lesson taught in many classrooms about writing. Create your main idea; then outline your three supporting ideas.

The Series of Stories: If there is any lesson I have learned through the observation of championship messages, most viewed Ted Talks, and memorable keynotes, it's this: you can share a series of similar stories connected by one theme, but what works even better is a series of stories that are chapters from one story and show how a person grew. In the speech about "just being you/let your light shine", my coach helped me craft three stories that each have the same message/theme. In contrast, in my speech called "I Am Scared", I shared a chronological set of stories from my life that showed how I evolved my feeling of being afraid from a debilitating force into a motivating factor. When I was preparing my keynote on developing your personal drive, my coach advised me to open with three stories about three different people who shared what drives them (similar stories connected by a theme). Then, I shared a few chapters from my life that detail what has driven me (a series of stories that demonstrate how a person grew).

The Countdown: From the 7 Habits of Highly Effective People to Jack Canfield's 65 Success Principles, numeric lists have become a road map for growth and achievement.

Preparing for a talk to a visiting troupe of educators from Hong Kong, one school leader I coached shared six factors that make for an exceptional high performing school: afterwards, he was invited to travel to China to share his talk.

The Acronym: It was in the second grade when I was I first introduced to the nine planets through a mnemonic device: My Very Educated Mother Just Served Us Nine Pickles. It's a nine-word sentence in which the first letter of each word matches the first letter of each of the nine planets. Years later, it's still stuck in my head (even though scientists now say that Pluto is not a planet; no more pickles.) Mnemonic devices are tools you can use to help improve your ability to remember something. In other words, it's a memory technique to help your brain better encode and recall important information. It's a simple shortcut that helps us associate the information we want to remember with an image, a sentence, or a word.

The Rules of E.N.G.A.G.E.M.E.N.T. is clearly an acronym, each letter standing for one of the Ten Rules to Rule the Stage! That acronym not only helps me to remember the information I want to share, but also, it helps me to remember the order in which I want to present that information. Order is key. And so is your audience's ability to follow your ideas.

These tools are effective. Brain research shows that we are inclined and designed to follow a sequence. In cognitive psychology, sequence learning is inherent to human ability because it is an integral part of conscious and unconscious learning. According to Ritter and Nerb, *"The order in which material is presented can strongly influence what is learned, how fast performance increases, and sometimes even whether the material is learned at all."*

Now here's the summary statement for the speech I shared earlier in this chapter: If you want people to pay attention to you, just be you.

In closing, compose a clear message and create a sequence of ideas or stories because that will help your audience to pay attention to you.

Take a moment now to reflect on the structure of one of your past, current, or future presentations. Then follow these steps:

Write a summary of your message in a 10-12 word sentence:

_____

_____

_____

_____

_____

_____

Make a list of the 3 or more chapters/talking points in your presentation. Summarize each chapter in just six words:

_____

_____

_____

_____

_____

_____

When your thoughts are easy to follow, your listeners will follow you.

Chapter 13:
Express Your Emotions

Emphasize and Emote: The way you deliver your words will create an impact. I said this earlier: never memorize your presentation; just practice it every chance you get. But what I will recommend is that after you prepare your message, you should then write it down, type it up, print it out, punch three holes in it, and put it in a binder (or as I like to call it: a speech book). Why? For several reasons, many of which I will outline shortly. But the most essential reason for typing, printing, and putting your words in a binder is to have a canvas on which you will "mark" the way you deliver those words. That I will elaborate on later. But first I want to address the habit of reading your notes.

Even though the goal is to speak without your notes, it's okay to have them, just like it's okay to have teleprompters. Although, I must say that teleprompters have become crutches. Some presenters depend on these teleprompters too much, forsaking the oh-so-more effective prep time. Instead of preparing for their presentation, they just show up to read. That may explain why TED Talk organizers did away with the teleprompter. In the defense of many teleprompter users though, I will admit that television producers and event coordinators have created the pressure of exact timing, but that can be practiced as well (I'll get to that before the end of the book.)

Now don't get me wrong, I'm not against people reading exact words and doing so in a precisely timed format. After all, I admire one of the greatest talkers in modern history: former President Barack Obama. If you watch his second Inaugural Address, you may notice him, just before he speaks, opening his speech book and then turning the pages as he proceeds. One news anchor reported that Obama had been working on the speech since December before the delivery in January. And yet, he still read. He's also had teleprompters positioned near many of his podiums. Despite the trap of monotony that often occurs when people read (think of those read-alouds in your high school English class), each time Obama read, he did so with his trademark passion; that's the product of preparation. If you prepare to read with passion, you can engage your listeners by the way you read. Teleprompters and scripts are not the problem. Rather they are the canvas.

It's okay to have that canvas for a few reasons:

1. It can help you to memorialize your words; you never know when you will have to deliver that presentation again. Can you imagine delivering a message so powerfully that you are asked to deliver it again at a later date only to forget exactly how you said it. Imagine trying to recreate the construction of those close-to-perfect words, only to realize that they are gone. And yes, it's your message, so you'll be able to find words nearly close to what you said, but it could be like starting from scratch. It's one thing to revise what you said to improve upon it; it's another thing to have to recreate it.

    On another note, you may want to memorialize your words, not only for the next verbal delivery, but also for the possibility of a published delivery. Yes, your message could be shared with audiences too far away or too plentiful for you to reach. I learned from a webinar hosted by the highly successful youth speaker Josh Shipp that a publication of your message (whether it be a book, blog, or article) is a powerful tool to create because it can reach more lives than you are capable of doing in person, regardless of how many stages you speak from. Also, publishing your words is a powerful tool that can be used to create amazing opportunities for you. If you believe your message is powerful and valuable, then don't be selfish. As Darren LaCroix taught me; don't limit your message to a one stage experience; memorialize it. Why share with a few what you can potentially share with many?

2. Right before your presentation, you can review your notes. I'm reminded of the many events I've attended where the speaker

placed her notes under her seat and then read through them before stepping to a podium.

3. During your presentation, just in case you forget what you prepared to say, you can refer to and read from your notes. Just make sure that if you do that, make eye contact and project your voice. And before you ever step in front of that audience, if you're going to read from your notes, read it so many times during practice that the words will become so internalized that you will know how to finish every sentence without looking down at the paper, across at the teleprompter, or back at the Powerpoint slide.

To help you even further, I recommend the same strategy I encouraged my wife to use when she hosted a high school graduation. It's the same strategy I recommend to all speakers who bring their speech books to the podium. If you are going to bring your script to the podium, then beforehand, print it in a very large font, possibly size 24; this will help you see your words, especially in dim lighting or extremely bright stage lighting. Then, triple or quadruple the space between the lines; this will prevent you from losing your space or repeating a line that was too close to the next. Next, end each page (and there will be a lot of pages depending on the length of the presentation) with a complete sentence; this will prevent you from flipping pages in the middle of a sentence, which could not only be a distraction to you, but also to your audience.

You should write it all down. And then, if you want your words to live and breathe the emotions and emphasis that you want your audience to experience, then you must follow this next step: "Mark Your Script". That's a theater term, but it's also a public speaking strategy. It means taking your typed speech or your prepared words, and doing the following: underline, color-code, circle, and/or highlight your key words. These are the words you want to emphasize that will tap into your audience's emotions. When speaking in front of others, we often use filler words, but in this case, I'm talking about using "feeler" words. Identify those emotional words and then breathe life into those words. Make your listeners "feel" you. Don't just say what you mean, but also speak the way you feel.

Also, identify those particular words that convey new ideas and new thoughts, and then emphasize those words. Select those words that are essential to the meaning of your message, words you want your listeners to remember because of their importance to your message, and then emphasize them. All of this must be done on purpose and with intent. You must intentionally "Mark Your Words" to Move Your Crowd. Have you ever been moved by someone else's words? How would it make you feel to have that same ability to move a crowd?

Mark my words: you can do it!

Sadly, my best friend's grandmother passed away. I went to the funeral to support Scott and his family. As I listened to the rabbi pay tribute, I was amazed by the movement of his words.

I watched his words shed a tear into our eyes.

I witnessed his words crack a smile onto our mouths.

I observed his words stiffen our upper lips.

Mark my words: He moved us.

But his words were not the cause, not entirely anyway. It is often believed that words are magical. But that is not true. The way you can deliver those words is what creates the magic. But what is it that certain speakers do to make their words come alive and breathe emotions into our souls? How do they do that to us? Well, that's just it: they do it to us by using "US". US, or rather U.S., stands for a simple strategy that you can implement to help you deliver with emotional and emphatic impact. US: Underline and Separate.

But before you can Underline and Separate, you have to know what to Underline and Separate. You have to feel it. When I asked a coaching client how he felt about the way he delivered his speech, he responded with an evaluation: "I stumbled on a few words. It took me awhile to get to my point. I'd give myself a 4 out of 10."

"No. I'm not asking you how well you did. I'm asking you about your feelings. I am asking about your emotional state."

"I felt okay."

I asked him to try describing how he felt again, to tell me more; to elaborate; to emote. You must emote. You must be clear and specific about the feelings you want to convey so you can determine how to express them if you want to move us.

As you prepare to speak, you should ask yourself three questions:

1. What emotions do you want to feel when you share your message?

2. What emotions do you want your audience to feel while they listen to your message?

3. How can you "mark" those emotions?

Research shows that there are six emotions that are universally recognized all over the world: sad, mad, scared, glad, surprised, and disgusted. Make it a goal to express a combination of 2 to 3 of those emotions each time you speak.

Most people can tell you what they want their audience to know from their words, but only some tend to give enough attention to how they want their listeners to feel through their words. Begin with that thought and get in touch with those feelings. Then put your words on paper and use "US" to mark your words.

Marking your words is a practice of underlining the words in your presentation that evoke an emotion and/or emphasize an essential idea. It also includes drawing a slant wherever you plan to pause for effect, in essence, separating the words. I have found that the most transformational and inspirational speakers are experts at emphasizing and emoting words and pausing emphatically and dramatically. And while that ability is natural for some, it can be strategic for everyone. So use "US". Underline and Separate.

If you want to move the crowd, you have to plan how you want them to move before you can make them move. Don't just plan what to say. Plan how to say it. That passion is pivotal. Mark these words: *"This is something you may have heard a number of times, but very few people understand what the word passion implies. The word itself, 'passion,' derives from the Latin root 'pati' — which means 'to suffer.' The veracity in this linguistic statement lies in the fact that passion is what moves you to persevere at something despite fear, unhappiness or pain. It is the determination and motivation to push through suffering for the sake of an end goal. What is more — this kind of motivation has an actual source in the brain. A recent study published in the Journal of Neuroscience has identified the part of the brain that is activated during motivated activities — the ventral striatum, in combination with the amygdala (known as the brain's emotional center). Researchers observed that the ventral striatum was activated in proportion to how motivated a person felt: the higher the degree of motivation, the higher the activation level."* (Malini Mohana).

Our brains are activated by passion. And that passion, your passion, touches our hearts. And that activity begins by identifying the emotion and the emphasis in your words, and then Underlining and Separating those words. Mark your words. That's what works for the speakers who move you. Throughout the service, the rabbi moved us with his passion. By the end of our coaching session, my client was moved by his newly "marked" passion.

The words are important, but the passion is pivotal. The passion is even magical when it is transferred from the speaker's marks to the audience's hearts.

Mark your emotions:

Words tell us. Passion touches us.

Words mean something. Passion moves someone.

When you mark your emotions, you move your crowds.

Many people will listen to and watch a powerful speaker, and respond, "Wow! He's such a talented speaker!" or "Wow! She is such a gifted speaker!" And while there is some truth to that: some people do have a natural gift, but like any other successful person, talent is enriched and propelled by craft.

The greatest talkers not only craft what they want to say beforehand, but they also craft how they want to say it beforehand. Speaking off the top of one's head is a skill and a highly respected skill, but if I may compare it to hip-hop music; freestyling is a gift and a rightfully respected talent, but the top of the music industry is not filled with freestylers; rather, it is populated by those who spend a great deal of time composing a song. Michael Jackson and Prince had distinct studio approaches, but both were legends because they were craftsmen. And I go back to President Obama: he had a speech book on hand, yes, but he had weeks of preparation beforehand to craft his delivery. And on a less famous note, I have on great authority from my good friend, mentor, and TEDX organizer Cathey Armillas, that all those who have graced the inside of the red circle (where all TED Talkers stand to deliver their speeches) spent months crafting, revising, and "marking" their words.

Here's an exercise for you in "marking the words" to help you understand and develop this technique further. First, read an excerpt from my book "Beyond Limitations". It's presented twice, once without the marks, because I am inviting you to mark the words the way you "feel" them. (Go ahead, you can write in the book.) And then, I'll share with you how I marked my words, (which may come in handy when I finally decide to record an audiobook version).

Task #1: Underline or highlight in yellow any words or phrases that you think help emphasize an important meaning. These are words you might say a little louder, a little lower, or a little slower so that your listeners get the point that this is something important to understand.

Task #2: Underline twice or highlight in red any words or phrases that you feel help express an emotion that sets the mood of the message. These are words you might speak with anger, fear, jubilation, worry, etc. so that your listeners can feel or sense the same emotion.

Task #3: Draw a diagonal line between words to indicate when you want to pause. Draw two diagonal lines to indicate a longer pause.

Task #4: Use a dotted line underneath any words or phrases that you want to say a little bit slower than usual.

Everything in my life points to the fact that I should have stopped by now. Everything in my life points to the fact that I should have been another statistic, but that didn't happen. I could have become frustrated, defeated, demoralized, but that didn't happen. I became the exception to the rule. And now I aim to make the exception the rule.

How did you mark my words?

Now let me share with you how I marked my words:

Everything in my life /points to the fact/ that I should have stopped by now. Everything in my life /points to the fact/ that I should have been/ another statistic,/ but that didn't happen. I could have become frustrated, defeated, demoralized, /but that didn't happen. I became the exception to the rule. And now/ I aim to make/ the exception the rule.

When it comes to marking your words, there's no right or wrong phrase to underline or highlight. I might highlight a different phrase than you. That's fine. What really matters is that no matter which words or phrases you identify as important to the meaning and emotions of the message, that you complete the task: highlight, underline, or color-code those words.

This is the same technique people use when they read bedtime stories to children. Even though they do not physically mark up the children's books, they are marking those words as they read. How else do you explain dad's intonations when he speaks in the Big Bad Wolf's voice? That's why children don't forget those stories, and then grow up to read those same stories with the same animated delivery to their own children.

If your goal is to deliver your message in a way that will make others remember you, in a way that makes people feel what you say, (not just hear your message, but feel your message), then don't just prepare WHAT you want to say, but also prepare HOW you want to say it. Identify those emphatic and expressive words and then prepare to say them the way you mean them and the way you feel them. Public Speaking is a strategy by design. And when it is done methodically, it is a strategy designed to compel people to pay attention to you.

Chapter 14:
Note Your Research

Notes and research will make you an expert; your content is just as important as your delivery. The great philosopher Aristotle was an architect of composition and persuasion. He laid out his blueprint just the way modern-day speakers are accustomed to doing it: in three parts. He argued that if you want to influence your audience, you need to use the three appeals: Ethos, Pathos, and Logos.

Ethos is about appealing to your listeners' perception of you as a reliable source of information. When they know they can believe you, they are more likely to pay attention to you. How credible do you want others to believe you are? How knowledgeable do you want others to believe you are? How believable do you want others to believe you are? Your answer to those questions are established by your appeal to ethos. When I talk about the art of engaging your listeners, I reference my membership to Toastmasters International; I highlight competing for the World Championship of Public Speaking; I mention delivering a Ted Talk; I mention that I coach clients on how to improve their communication and presentation skills; I speak about being an English teacher. I talk about my credentials, my background, and my expertise. Now be careful, don't go up there and brag about yourself because people can be turned off by a person who talks about himself too much. Don't go over the top about who you are and what you have accomplished. Instead, develop a story or two that will reveal your character profile rather than share a brag sheet that exposes your ego. Just say enough to let them know who you are. And if you're going to be introduced, don't give the host too much to say either. For example, I enjoy telling the story about how I failed to win the World Championship in 2014 because not only does it reference how far I was able to advance in the craft of composing and delivering a message that gets people to pay attention, but also it reveals that, like others, I still have some lessons to master.

Who are you? What qualifies you to speak on your topic? What's the story along your journey that chronicles how you became qualified?

Furthermore, pay attention to your non-verbal language because what you communicate non-verbally impacts the impression you make upon others and, as a result, their inclination to pay attention to you. The Harvard Study of Communications, as reported by Amando Johns Vaden *(The Nuts and Bolts of First Impressions, August 2015),* said that it only takes seven seconds for you to make a first impression on another human being, only seven seconds. Only 7% of the first impression has anything to do with the words that you say. 55% of a first impression is visual: how you look, how you dress, how you stand, how you shake a hand, and how you make solid eye contact. 38% of that first impression is determined by one's tone (how you speak your words). That leaves 2% for what you say. Your non-verbal language speaks volumes. Pay attention, very acutely, to how you communicate non-verbally during those first seven seconds; again, it will affect the way your listeners perceive you. That will impact your ethos.

That includes paying attention to your personal appearance. My wife is my stylist. She picks out everything I wear before I deliver a presentation. Heck, she picks out everything I wear whenever I leave the house. I rely on her to do that for me because image contributes to ethos too. First impressions impact how people listen to you. So before you take the floor to speak, put a lot of thought into how you want your introduction, your reputation, your appearance, and your image to strengthen the reception of your message.

Pathos: What do they want? You may be the one on stage; you may be the one who has the floor, but the reason why they will want to listen to you is because they're waiting to see what is in it for them. What can you offer to them that they want or need? That is why it so crucial to know, learn about, or survey your audience beforehand. When you know what makes them tick, and you speak to that, then they are more likely to pay attention to you.

When I watched the 2016 World Champion of Public Speaking Darren Tay Wen Jie, I noticed that he asked the audience to think about the inner bullies that were holding them back. I'm sure many of us can relate to beating ourselves up and putting ourselves down and would like to break that cycle so that we can push ourselves forward.

When I watched TED Talker and educator Kandice Sumner talk about the underserved black and brown children in hers and many other public schools, I was floored by her last line, "What is a carpenter with no tools? What is an actress with no stage? What is a scientist with no laboratory? What is a doctor with no equipment? I'll tell you...They're my kids. Shouldn't they be your kids too?" She tapped into what I'm sure is a desire among many: to see all of OUR children achieve. Earlier, she said, "If you're a human being, DONATE...time, money, resources..." Are we not all human beings, with hearts, with compassion, human beings who want to feel like what we can do will make a difference?

What I do for you may benefit you, but will it validate me? Isn't that something that many of your listeners want or need? Ms. Sumner put the focus on us. As a communicator, do the same; don't put all of your focus on you; instead, put your focus on the YOU's sitting in your audience. Connect your message to what they want and what they need because they are the reason you are speaking. That will increase the value and the reception of your message. This lesson was reinforced for me years ago while sitting in the barbershop.

As I sat in the chair at the barbershop, I had visions of Michael Jackson dancing in my head to the beat of "The Way You Make Me Feel". Now that may sound strange, but let me explain. I was listening to a conversation between two barbers about the newest barber in the shop. He was a young kid who boasted about the enormous number of customers he was going to have knocking down his door in just the next two weeks. He believed that the way to make that happen was by winning people over with his charm: "Just talk to them and make them think you are friendly and cool."

The two other, more experienced barbers said that this kid would never succeed in the business if he didn't learn the essential lesson: **It's not about you. It's about how you make others feel.** It's not about the small talk you make about the things that interest you that may interest others too; it's not about making other people like you; and it's not about how they feel about you. That's not what builds a following. What builds a following is how you make people feel about themselves. It's about investing in them. I told my barber that in all my years of getting haircuts, I had never stuck with one barber. I may have stuck with one barbershop, but never with one barber, not until he cut my hair. And when I reflect on why that is the case, I realized that it's not because he cuts hair any better than most of the barbers I've been to; it's because when he cuts my hair, he takes the time to get to know me. And he treats my sons the same way. The experience in his chair is about the person in the chair. As a matter of fact, my barber said that he actually never talks to a customer the first time he ever cuts that person's hair..."because the focus should not be about the way you feel about me, but rather the way I make you feel about you." But after that, he will engage you in conversations about you.

This is a universal rule. If you want to be an engaging communicator or an effective leader, don't focus on what the audience thinks about you. That usually makes speakers nervous and leaders ineffective. And it distracts speakers and leaders from the primary goal: to help others. If the people you aim to help, love the way you make them feel about themselves, then they will love to listen to you...again and again.

So here's a rule: When you are preparing your talk or your meeting, ask yourself, "How do I want my audience to feel about themselves after I'm done? What can I say to make them feel that way?". When you focus on how they feel, you seal the deal. So what do you know about what your audience wants? What can you talk about to them, and how can you talk about it in such a way that makes them feel like the person speaking on stage is putting them center stage? Before you speak, do your homework: find out what you need to know about your audience, such as gender, age range, profession, past experiences with your topic, notable accomplishments, interests, and aspirations.

For example, when I talk about the need to develop your presentation skills, I mentioned money. Why? Because I haven't met a person yet who isn't interested in how to save more or make more money. When talking to the members of the National Society of Black Engineers, I highlighted the fact that the highest paid engineers are those who are required to have the following communication skills:

- Negotiates critical and controversial issues with top-level engineers and officers of other organizations and companies.
- Conducts presentations and may participate in media interviews.
- Represents their organization at important functions or conferences, including media interviews.

That list of communication skills can be applied to any profession in which there are people who want, desire, and/or need to increase their income. Is that what you want? And if so, is that desire to learn about making more money a logical desire or an emotional desire? If you want your audience to listen, tap into their emotions.

But money is not the only thing people want. Some people desire personal development. Some desire a healthier lifestyle. In the case of speaking in front of people, some people just want to be more comfortable and confident. Whatever the case may be, speak to what your audience emotionally desires. As reported by ISPO News in January 2015, *"'A major part of our brain is busy with automatic processes, not conscious thinking. A lot of emotions and less cognitive activities happen,' says behavioral economist George Loewenstein. Our brains usually run on autopilot, despite making us believe we know what we are doing. Thus, our subconscious explains our consumer behavior better than our conscious. 90 percent of all purchasing decisions are not made consciously, experts claim. Or put it this way: brands and products that evoke our emotions, like Apple, Coca-Cola or Nivea, always win."*

Whether it be buying a product, a service, or a message, listeners are more likely to be driven by their desire. If you want your message to have more appeal, then appeal to how your listeners feel.

But as influential as Ethos and Pathos are, they are just two-thirds of a powerful combination; the last third is my real focus though.

Logos is all about appealing to your audience's thought-process. After all, the most common goal when we talk is to get the other person or people to think differently; keyword: think. After all, the most common goals when we listen are to have our minds stimulated and to learn something new. So give your audience something to think about and expand their knowledge; doing so will increase their alertness.

Furthermore, audiences are much more engaged when they know that what you have to say has been backed up by research. That helps you become and be seen as the expert on the topic. For my Ted Talk titled "The World is Watching", I followed my coach's advice to include researched data. I underlined those researched notes for you.

I need to start by taking a moment to take this all in! I'm standing in the middle of the proverbial red circle, the same place where thousands of speakers have stood to deliver their Ted Talks, the same red circle that is watched at a rate of 1.5 million times a day! Wow! That thought just blows my mind. And when I told my good friend Cathey about this Ted Talk opportunity, she said, "Don't worry. relatively speaking, there will only be a small number of people in the room who will actually see your talk."

Whew!

"However, 98% of the people who might see your talk will watch it online because it will be on the internet forever, for anyone to see! So remember when I said, 'Don't worry.' I lied. Worry. Worry enough to work hard enough to come up with an idea worth spreading."

Talk about pressure! But I'm here, me, this poor kid from Brooklyn, because I have an idea worth spreading.

Pause to Ponder: Quantifiable evidence can add an element of surprise that engages your listeners. And usually, numbers don't lie.

But forget about me. What about you? What idea do you have worth spreading? And notice that I didn't ask you "if you have an idea worth spreading, but rather "what" idea you have worth spreading because I am certain that each and every one of you has something of value to share. The question is with whom are you sharing your ideas, your photos, and your videos? And why should you share those ideas, photos, videos, and posts with more people whom you don't even know? Do you share with just your circle of friends? And if so, how big or small is your circle of friends? Though that doesn't really matter because no matter how big or small your circle of friends is, there's an entire sphere of influence, an entire world out there that has access to see what you share, no matter what privacy settings you have on: from the college admissions board at the university you're applying to, or to the human resources department at the Fortune 500 company you're interviewing at, or the thousands of people on dating websites looking to take you out to the movies. As a matter of fact, <u>I recently received an email the other day from FortuneMagazine.com about being selected for a coaches council. When I asked them why I was selected, they said, "We've been looking at what you've been sharing on-line."</u> Wow! That confirmed it. Anybody can see what you share.

Pause to Ponder: Personal anecdotes can add a genuine appeal because no one can debate what you say happened to you.

That's when I had this image of being a young boy watching The Honeymooners. Now, I don't know how many of you know of or remember that show, but <u>there was one episode when the main character Ralph Kramden had an idea to sell a kitchen utensil that does everything. But he didn't want to go door-to-door selling the utensil. Instead, he wanted to record an infomercial on live T.V. He was ready. He was confident! But he was scared when he learned how many people would be watching.</u> Jackie Gleason, the actor who played Ralph, made that scene one of the most comical moments on television I have ever seen. But the thought of everyone watching you may not actually be a very comical feeling at all...that is, unless you want to share something funny. But whether you want to share something funny, serious, or share-worthy, if you knew, as you should, that the whole world could see what you share, what would you want them to see?

Pause to Ponder: References to pop culture moments add validity because of the sheer volume of people who viewed it just like you.

Now that's not an invitation to be a host of your own reality show, but the reality is that if you have a Facebook account, an Instagram account, a Youtube channel, or any other social media account, then you are already the star of your own reality show. So again, if you knew the entire world could see what you share, what would you show? More importantly, and this is the essential question related to the idea I want to spread today: If you knew the entire world had access to see what you show, then how might that affect the quality of what you share?

My conclusion is that it would enhance the quality of what you share because my premise is this: the bigger the audience the greater the pressure to perform better. So if you want a better performance, better results, or a greater impact on you or the world around us, then increase your reach beyond the people you already know because the size of the audience tends to push us to present work that is well-received by most of those people.

Pause to Ponder: Making an argument begs for supporting evidence. Aim to present a premise worth arguing and presenting.

I first began to think of this idea right after I became the principal of a Brooklyn high school for journalism. Journalism, the craft of sharing and spreading ideas and information. Shortly after I arrived, I decided that I didn't just want my students to share their ideas and work with only their classmates in the Journalism elective. And I didn't just want the students in my school to only share their ideas and work with only the other students in the school who might read the school newspaper. So I dropped the idea of a traditional print school newspaper and decided to produce an online digital newspaper that students could

use to write about global issues on a global platform.
I wanted to give my students a bigger audience because I believed that a bigger audience would improve the quality of their performance.

The bigger the audience the greater the pressure to perform better.

But how did I know this would work? Because of the capuchin monkeys.

In a 2009 study of capuchin monkeys, researchers put a group of monkeys to one side and a solo monkey to the other side. And then they gave the monkeys the task of searching for food. And though they found in several observations that both the group of monkeys and the solo monkey were able to complete the task, they found that the group of monkeys were able to complete the task three times faster. Now some would say "Of course. There were more monkeys to search for the food." And while that is a valid point, the group of monkeys were also able to find their food three times faster because of social facilitation, otherwise known as the audience effect, which states that people perform better in the presence of other people. This is similar to the Yerkes Dodson Law, which states that the mere presence of other people enhances your performance.

The bigger the audience the greater the pressure to do better.

Another study was done in 1920 when a group of people were asked to create a list of words in response to a given word. I remember playing a game like that in elementary school. We would take out a sheet of paper, write at the top of the sheet a word like, "supercalifragilisticespialidocious", and then create our list of words. It was a fun game. I challenge you to try it. The study showed that 93% of the participants created a larger list when in the presence of other people than those who did it alone.

The bigger the audience the greater the pressure to perform better.

Pause to Ponder: Many studies have been conducted. Search for a potentially unfamiliar study that gives your listeners something new to know.

This reminds me of a recent night out I had with a group of friends to play a game called "escape the room". You're locked in a room for 60 minutes. You have to find the clues and the keys to get out. For days leading up to it, I was dreading doing this because I thought I was going to be completely inept at helping my friends escape the room. But the pressure of being in the presence of my five friends pushed me to step up my game. And while I didn't contribute as much as some of the others, I did better than I expected.

The bigger the audience the greater the pressure to perform better.

But had I been in the room alone, an audience of none, or with just one other friend, an audience of one, I might not have escaped the room. Smaller audiences lead to smaller results.

Pause to Ponder: That was another personal anecdote to give the audience something to think about.

That brings me to the school system. As an educator for over 20 years and a student for much longer, here is what I have noticed: schools exist on the premise of an audience of one (the teacher), or at most, a limited audience of some (the classmates). That's a disservice to our students and the world around us. Think about it: some of the greatest stories never told are sitting on the desk of an English teacher, only for her to see. Some of the greatest solutions and arguments to the world's most complex problems, are sitting on a history teacher's desk or in a science teacher's lab, only for him to see. And some of the greatest works of art and innovative ideas never to be shared are sitting on the desk of an art teacher, only for her to see. That's a disservice to our students and to a world that can benefit from what our students and ourselves can contribute.

The bigger the audience the greater the pressure to perform better.

I learned that in high school. My English teacher, Dr. Sylvia Weinberger, gave us a writing assignment. Our task was to write an essay on a topic of our choice. Being a kid from a neighborhood where everyone listened to hip-hop, except me, I wrote about de-mystifying the myth that there is such a thing as black music and white music. I was proud of that essay. And Dr. Weinberger liked it too. And she liked five other essays, so much so that she said she wanted us to share our work, not just in front of the class, and not just in front of the school, but in front of a live studio audience at WNYW Radio in New York City. The thought scared me. Dr. Weinberger, "Can I not do this?" She said, "I want you to do this because the experience will help you." So then we, the Radio Six as I like to call us, revised, rewrote, and recomposed those essays. And I'm proud to share that we did a pretty good job. And we didn't even catch a case of stage fright.

Pause to Ponder: That was another personal anecdote to give the audience something to think about.

But I can't say the same for a teacher who was afraid to be the advisor for an online digital newspaper. She was concerned that her students' work would be a reflection of her. So none of those students posted any articles until this teacher realized that the bigger the audience the greater the pressure to push her to do a better job of teaching her students how to do a better job. They were very proud of their work.

That reminds me of one of the toughest, most defiant kids I ever worked with. He was standing in front of his English class because he wanted to ask his teacher why his work wasn't on the board. He actually put a lot of work into it. But it wasn't the grade that mattered. What mattered was the audience. In this day and age, grades are not a strong enough motivator. A promotion is not a strong enough motivator. A pat on the back to say, "Good job Marc. I like your work," is not a strong enough motivator. A bigger audience is a strong motivator. Tell me I'm doing a good job, in front of other people, and I'll do a better job in front of more people.

The bigger the audience the greater the pressure to perform better.

Pause to Ponder: That was another personal anecdote to give the audience something to think about.

So I asked a group of students, "If your teacher told you that every major assignment would be posted on-line and while it would be graded using a traditional rubric, you could also earn more points for your level of Engagement on social media. The more likes, the more shares, the more views, the more follows, the more positive comments from people you don't already know, the more points you earn towards your grade. How do you think that would affect the quality of your work?"

While some of the students said, "That sounds way too extreme for me!", they all agreed that the project would push them to do better work.

Pause to Ponder: Testimonials serve as proof that others agree with your argument. Conduct a survey as you construct your message.

So I propose that all schools create courses that expand their classrooms beyond the four walls of the school. Help our children develop the transferable and essential skills of marketing, promoting, branding, and creating content worth spreading. Give our students and ourselves a bigger audience.

The bigger the audience the greater the pressure to perform better.

Studies show that a bigger audience leads people to share things that make them look better, use more positive language, and reframe negative events to make themselves look less bad.

Pause to Ponder: That's another reference to a study that supports the message.

That describes the profile and social media presence that I want to help our students and ourselves to develop. The whole world is watching anyway. So if the entire world already will have access to see what our children, in many cases, are irresponsibly posting, then let's take this as an opportunity to show the world something better. This would increase the value and the impact of social media and of a social media generation that will one day be the leaders of our world.

This is also an opportunity to equip ourselves with the valuable skill of not only attracting the attention of others, but also of engaging and holding the attention of millions of others. How else can we build our businesses, put seats in our arenas, sell our products and services, rally participants for our marches, or get billions of people to watch cat videos on our Youtube channels? But just getting likes and shares is not enough to teach our children. We have to teach them how to engage their viewers. <u>Nowadays, the financial and social value of what we share is not measured by the number of people who see what we share, but rather by how long they watch what we share. Thirty seconds of sustained attention is now the unit of measure of engagement on social media.</u> Just imagine if everyday, you could engage one new person every thirty seconds with what you share, you'd have a new audience of 2,880 viewers every day. Imagine what the potential of an audience of that size can do to push you to create ideas worth spreading. So, if you don't already know more than 2,880 people, then what are you waiting for? Increase your reach beyond the people you don't already know. Expand your virtual community to sustain our future because the bigger the audience, the greater the pressure for you to perform better...because #TheWorldIsWatching

Pause to Ponder: The use of numbers was a strategy to encourage listeners to think about how they sustain attention in thirty seconds on social media. Invite your listeners to think, if you want them to pay attention to you.

For a TED Talk, one has to do the research. The same is true for other presentations too. Make it your goal to learn more so you can teach more because people tend to listen more to others who know more.

One day, I sat through a ten-hour City Council meeting. There were a lot of people there giving a lot of different testimonies about things they were emotional about. They were all heartfelt messages, but the testimonial that stood out the most was delivered by this one man who reinforced the stories told by others with facts and the statistics. This time, facts and statistics stood out because on this occasion, he was the only one who took that approach; even though that is usually a boring strategy, in this case, it made him unique. And when he walked out of the room, many people stopped him to say, "Wow! That was great! It looks like you did a lot of research." He replied, "Yes. That's right. Because that's what we're supposed to do."

With that said, research is not just limited to facts and statistics. The gentleman I just referenced made such an impression because his approach was a break from the norm. Unfortunately, in most cases, the norms are numbers, facts, and citations about scientific studies. But that's not the only type of researched data. Your story is your researched data too. Your personal observations are your researched data too. It's all notable information that may be valuable to someone else. It's your purpose to give them information that they did not know. Often, I will ask audiences if they know what inspired Steve Jobs to create the I-pod; when most people respond that they don't know, I tell them that's the same answer they want from their audiences. That creates the opportunity for you to advance their learning with your knowledge and/or to advance their insight with your findings. Then combine that information with personal stories, and what you will have is the key to getting people to pay attention.

I'm intrigued by brain research and the cognitive sciences, so I reference my findings a lot. But that's not my area of expertise. Therefore, I do research so that I can ENGAGE my audience. And what I've learned and reinforced to others is that it is very important to share something new to know or to share a new twist on what people may already know. It's important to show that you know what you're talking about, either because you experienced it, you observed it, or you researched it. When your listeners know that what you have to say is backed up by research and discovery, they will be much more engaged. Furthermore, you want to present them with information that pushes your audience to think. The more they think, the more they are engaged.

In an article by Lecia Bushak, she noted the following: A study that was published in the journal Neuron *"found that people who were curious about a subject learned more and remembered more information than others. So instead of being a punishable and risky quality, curiosity 'may put the brain in a state that allows it to learn and retain any kind of information, like a vortex that sucks in what you are motivated to learn, and also everything around it,' Dr. Matthias Gruber of the University of California at Davis."*

"Perhaps most significantly, when curiosity is stimulated, it is linked to increased activity in the hippocampus, which is the part of the brain that makes new memories. So the hippocampus seems to put the brain in a state in which you are more likely to learn and retain information, even if that information is not of particular interest or importance," Dr. Charan Ranganath, another author of the study and lead investigator, said in the press release. In an interview with The Guardian, Ranganath said that "once you light that fire of curiosity, you put the brain in a state that's more conducive to learning. Once you get this ramp-up of dopamine, the brain becomes more like a sponge that's ready to soak up whatever is happening." (MedicalDaily.com, October 2014).

As you prepare to speak, do your research and make it a goal to teach at least one new thing that makes your audience think about something they did not know. Doing so will make you the expert that others will want to pay attention to.

Chapter 15:
Track Your Timing

Timing is Everything and Pausing is Powerful.

During the 2016 season of the Toastmasters International Contest, I competed with a speech called, "I Am Scared!" During Round 1, a club member informed me that he thought I went over the time limit. The contest rules state that the speech must be 5-7 minutes long; speakers are allowed a 30 second window on either end. Any speech less than 4 minutes and 30 seconds and any speech more than 7 minutes and 30 seconds is automatically disqualified. In that first round, I finished with nanoseconds left to spare and advanced to Round 2. During Round 2, I ad-libbed a little before bringing my speech to a close. My good friend John said that my fate would depend on when the timekeeper started the clock. By a narrow margin, I beat the clock and advanced to Round 3. While preparing for that 3rd Round, John and others advised me on what to cut so that I could finish the speech without coming dangerously close to the time limit. Over the next few weeks, I made some revisions to a speech that when I originally composed it for a non-contest situation was 20 minutes long. Needless to say, the speech had already gone through some major cuts. But there was more to chop off. Prior to stepping onto the stage for Round 3, a fellow Toastmaster approached me and whispered, "Watch your time. Keep your eye on the red card." Clearly, I had worried many people during the first two rounds. But during Round 3, I was in a rhythm and a flow that orchestrated the right pacing and the right timing. I advanced to Round 4, confident that time would not be an issue. Nevertheless, I always practiced with my stopwatch. There were times when I hit 7:18; there were times when I exceeded 7:38. I concluded that my delivery relied heavily on my rhythm and pacing. And while there is truth to that, the word count matters too, but the syllable count matters more.

During the contest briefing for Round 4, I drew the eighth slot, which meant I had to wait nearly 52 minutes before I took the stage after the contest began. And there were still hours before the contest would start. So I made my way to the parking lot where I practiced again and again and again. For my first rehearsal, I practiced without the stopwatch...that was a mistake. For my second rehearsal, I noticed that I had forgotten to press START...that would turn out to be a regret. For the third rehearsal, I clocked in at 7:28...that was close, but I was comfortable being too close for comfort, though that is not my recommendation. Finally, the time had come; my name was called to step onto the stage. I was seven minutes and twenty-eight seconds away from quite possibly my second trip to the semi-finals of the World Championship of Public Speaking. As I was being introduced, a thought occurred: "Should I skip over that line: 'Scared to try something, or to say something, or to do something.' If I leave it out, it won't take away from the message...true, but I like the way the sequence of phrases sounds...keep it in there." I said the line the way it was originally written and then continued...time ticked away. Several minutes later, I included the new line that I had never used in a previous round of competition: "If you're gonna be scared, then be scared for the right reason"...time ticked away. Then I made an adjustment that referenced a speaker who had just presented minutes earlier (a technique that shows the kind of spontaneity that livens up a pre-packaged speech); I was fortunate to get a long laugh from the crowd...but the time was ticking away. Have you ever felt like you were running out of time?

Then something happened that never occurred during any practice I ever had: For months, I said the following words, in the same exact order...in the same exact way...in the same...

"And if you choose to be scared of the right thing, then you will find that you are no longer held back by your fears, but pushed forward by your fears; that you are no longer powerless to your fears, but empowered by your fears; and that you are no longer haunted by your fears, but that you are hoisted by your fears."

I always delivered those lines in that order, but in the moment, when my subconscious mind must have been aware of the seconds I had left, I unintentionally skipped to the last part of the sequence: "that you are no longer haunted by your fears, but that you are hoisted by your fears." In a split second, I returned to my conscious mind and I posed this (slow-motion) thought: "Should I keep going and close out the speech, or should I go back and say the other two parts of the phrase to achieve that rhetorical effect I was aiming for?" I made my decision...

I chose the rhetorical effect.

As the red card rose into my view, I sped up my rate to adjust, but I would not quit on my mission to say all the words I came to say, including conducting the crowd to repeat after me...three times: "I Am Scared!...I Am Scared!!...I Am Scared!!!"

I was done. The crowd applauded. I wiped away the sweat that had built up from the uncertainty of whether or not I had escaped running over time. I felt secure that I had finished just in time to beat the disqualification...until a fellow Toastmaster whispered to me, "I think you might have gone over." He said, "I think." He wasn't sure that I had. And then, I wasn't sure that I hadn't. Several minutes later, just before the Contest Chair read the results, he announced that there was one disqualification. I turned to the people at my table: "It's me. I went over."

I was right.

I cannot guarantee that I would have placed in the top three or even won the contest to advance to the semi-finals. But what I do know is that I eliminated myself...but by how much? Did I really want to know the answer to that question? Weeks later, I heard the audio when a fellow Toastmaster played it for me at a meeting. It seemed to indicate that I went over by nearly 20 seconds. That's so over time, that it hurt, but I was nowhere close to finishing the speech on time, so I could live with that. Then a few more weeks later, my buddy John, who had videotaped my presentation said that I actually went over by 7 seconds.

That was a tougher pill to swallow. A phrase cut here or there could have made a difference. That was a tough lesson to learn. Months later though, someone revealed a piece of news that became the toughest pill to swallow; her words got stuck in my throat, her revelation got tattooed on my brain. And it still stings to this day. When I shared my story at a Rules of Engagement workshop, someone else, who may very well had been a contest official at the time, shouted out that I actually went over by....one second....one second...that's heartbreaking: that's a word; that's a pause; that's a lesson learned. Toastmasters gives you a 30 second window to finish a speech which should be 5-7 minutes. I became comfortable in the window. That was a bad idea.

We often have time limits when we speak; even when it's not an official time limit, there's a limit to how much more people want to hear. As Aaron Beverly (2019 World Champion of Public Speaking) said in his 2016 contest speech, "Just because you say more doesn't mean people will remember what you say." No matter what you have to say, you will only have a limited amount of time to say it. That one-minute elevator pitch; that five-minute cold-call/sales pitch; that 5-7 minute speech; that 20-minute presentation; that two minute block of time when responding to interview questions; or those 3 minutes you have left to tell that story before your date starts regretting the evening, all have one thing in common: a time limit. And if you go over that time, significantly over that time, your audience may tune you out because there is nothing that people value more than their time. In Toastmasters, if you go over time, you will lose a contest. In any other situation, if you go over time, you may lose your audience.

Rule of Engagement: Whenever you speak, keep your eyes on the clock.

Sometimes though, the challenge is not going over time, but rather going under time. That can be just as bad because when you go significantly under the time given to you to talk, people might think, "Oh, he didn't really have that much to say." Or they might think that you didn't care enough to spend the time to prepare for them.

If it is your goal when you speak to draw your listeners in and keep them engaged, then it is in your best interest not to communicate that you don't value their time nor to communicate that you have little to offer to them. Instead, prepare mindfully for the time you will be given to speak to that audience. Whether it's a 20-minute business presentation, a 5 minute cold-call, or a 2-3 minute response during an interview, prepare with the time in mind. *"A time limit is an opportunity to hone and tailor your presentation to its most optimal. Do you have five minutes to present? You'd better make those five minutes count. That means distilling your material to its most impactful elements and focusing on that which you want your audience to think, do or feel."* (Deft Communications, "Be Aware of Your Time Limit", April 21, 2015).

Time is your tool; use it to build your capacity to engage. There are two tools you need to have with you when you practice your presentation: a stopwatch and a notepad. A third tool could be the word count feature on your PC, Mac, laptop, or tablet. Record how long it takes you to deliver your presentation. When it's a very long presentation, let's say 45 minutes to an hour or more, break the presentation up into several chunks. Practice the presentation in chunks and then record how long it takes you to deliver each chunk of your presentation. Then add up the time and check it against your time limit. If you find that you have too much material for the time given to you, then decide which portions you will cut out. Don't be stubborn about what you want to them to hear. Be strategic about how much they need to hear. Think of it as an artform. How can you chisel your message down to a shorter work of art? A colleague of mine wrote to me one morning about an opportunity to speak as a part of an esteemed group; she was invited to tell her story, but was told she would only have two minutes to share. She felt the pressure; pressure is what we use to find diamonds. Together, we condensed her tall-order tale into a two-minute gem. You can do the same, whether it be for a talk or an interview. Start with the extra words: usually adjectives, adverbs, or repetitive or redundant phrases; essentially, cut out any words that do not detract from your message. Or, as I was advised once by a member of my audience after a presentation, take out any extra anecdotes that you use to reinforce a point. Stories are great, but the second and third stories are not always necessary if your listeners get the point. Whatever you cut is your choice. Just cut something when time is of the essence, or else your audience will cut you off.

Then count your words before they count you out. During that contest season I referenced earlier, I wish I had remembered to keep count of my minutes and my words. Some sources state that on average, we speak 120-180 words per minute. How many words do you speak in a minute? There are apps now that can help you calculate your speaking and conversation rate. I recommend using those tools because that range of 120 to 180 words per minute indicates that in addition to the number of words you may use, the pacing of your delivery is a factor. One website, speechinminutes.com provides the following chart: (based on an average reading speed of 130 words per minute):

Words in 1 minute: 130	How many minutes does it take to speak 500 words: 3.8
Words in 2 minutes: 260	How many minutes does it take to speak 1000 words: 7.7
Words in 3 minutes: 390	How many minutes does it take to speak 1250 words: 9.6
Words in 4 minutes: 520	How many minutes does it take to speak 1500 words: 11.5
Words in 5 minutes: 650	How many minutes does it take to speak 1750 words: 13.5
Words in 10 minutes: 1300	How many minutes does it take to speak 2000 words: 15.4
Words in 15 minutes: 1950	How many minutes does it take to speak 2500 words: 19.2
Words in 20 minutes: 2600	How many minutes does it take to speak 5000 words: 38.5

You can use this source or one of the many other tools to help you with your time. You could also count the words in your manuscript. Or to be more precise, as it impacts your pacing, count your syllables. The syllable count is actually my recommended strategy. Words vary in length, but a syllable is a syllable. So count your syllables the next time you have to strategically prepare for a presentation.

However, since you are encouraged not to rely on precise wording, except in certain cases, the word and syllable count may not always be your best measuring stick. A more accurate measurement of your delivery time is a continuous timing of your delivery. After several run-throughs, calculate your average presentation time. If my average presentation rate for "I Am Scared" was 7:28, then I gave myself only a two-second window. That should have been too close for my comfort. But it wasn't, because of how I clocked in earlier during the week. On the Monday before the District Contest, I practiced my speech in front of a few co-workers. I clocked in twice at 6:51. I was feeling good. Note: We often speak slightly faster when we're actually presenting as compared to when we are practicing. It must be the adrenaline rush, the nerves, or just the desire to get it over with. Whatever the reason may be for an increased pace in front of the audience, the best way to prepare for the time you have to speak is tracking your average speaking time. Feeling comfortable at 6:51 (which was not my average speaking time), I added a line to accentuate my message. That was a gamble. And as you know by now, I took a chance only to lose an opportunity.

Don't lose your opportunities.

Don't lose your audience when you can win them over.

If you find that you have more to say, but not enough time allotted to say it, then take something out.

My friend and colleague Crystal only had two minutes to speak, but she had so many stories to share and so many details to the solution she had to offer. She had enough material for a TED Talk or an hour-long keynote. So she was frantic because she didn't know where to start her cuts nor how much to omit. Crystal cut out some of her childhood stories and some of the stories from raising her own children. She then cut out some of her descriptors, phrases that are there for emphasis, but could be omitted because their absence didn't take away from the meaning of her message. She cut enough, so precisely that she continues to receive invitations to speak to many audiences on the topic of education reform.

One of my clients spun his head crafting a speech on phubbing (the practice of ignoring one's companion or companions in order to pay attention to one's phone or other mobile device), only to chisel out a masterpiece of a talk about "getting ready to be ready". But the revisions included additions and the additional words became additional minutes. And we weren't even done yet with the changes. He was worried. And his concern was understandable. But if you ever find yourself worried about drafting too much material, tell yourself this: *"Stop. In the process of composing the message, do not fret over the time. If you do, it will stifle your creativity. Flesh out your message. And when the time comes, and when it is necessary to do so, then strip it down."* On the flipside, there are times when you will be expected to say more, speak for longer, or fill the time. A fellow Toastmaster who became a paid keynote speaker began to worry when he was invited to deliver a 60-minute version of a 5-7 minute speech. He did it. He won them over. If you find that you don't have enough information to fill the time, then add more.

There's usually something more we can add to emphasize, clarify, or support a point. Add more when necessary, but don't add so much that you feel like you have to spit it all out in a frenzy. Remember, it is better to engage people with everything you can say than to lose your audience with everything you wanted to say.

At that City Council meeting I referenced earlier, all of the registered speakers were given four minutes to speak. There was a digital timer on the wall. I remember this one woman who raced through her words. Her phrases tripped over each other. Her clauses barreled through her conjunctions. Her breath ran out of air. In the sound-blur, I didn't catch a word she said. She read so fast that no one understood. Frenzy on the part of the speaker makes it difficult to listen. Pace yourself.

I once heard that the mouth moves faster than the brain, but everything I've read says differently. Kelly Vandever, a presentation skills coach noted that the average person can comprehend at a rate up to 300 words per minute. That would seem that if we speak at a rate of 120-180 words per minute, that any listener can comprehend any speaker; and yet, there are many speakers, myself included, who have been advised to slow down. Why? It's because many of the things we say require more time for thought and reflection. People are not listening just to recognize the words, but to draw meaning from the message. If you want people to listen to you, don't just aim for your words to be heard. Aim for your message to be processed. Don't exhaust your listeners with words. Engage them with a strategically paced message.

And when you prepare your pace, don't forget to use your pause.

Your pause is powerful.

Your pause is dramatic.

Your pause is strategic.

When you pause, you allow yourself to self-reflect and to collect your thoughts. In Toastmasters International, members will count the number of ah's, um's, and er's in your speech. But outside of Toastmasters, there is no one who will officially count your fillers, but there are plenty of people who will comment on your use of them. Watch the next celebrity awards show; the acceptance speeches are filled with fillers. My advice: Cut down the fillers with a pause. The pause is your natural "ah-counter".

By the way, why do we use fillers? It's not because we want to; we don't even like the sound of them. We don't consciously choose to use the um's, er's, and ah's that plague our delivery. Subconsciously, we use these fillers as a means to give ourselves some extra time to think. Don't "fill" to think. Instead, pause to think. You'll sound better.

Culturally, as a human race, we also use these fillers because we have become uncomfortable with silence. In an article called "Our Fear of Silence" by George Hofmann for PsychCentral.com, the author notes: *"A study of 580 undergraduate students undertaken over six years, reported by Bruce Fell on The Conversation, shows that the constant accessibility and exposure to background media has created a mass of people who fear silence."* Furthermore, Mellissa Dahl reported for *NBCNews that "people who experienced the awkward silence reported feeling 'distressed, afraid, hurt, and rejected,' according to the paper published in the Journal of Experimental Social Psychology."* Silence can be so uncomfortable. Have you ever gone on a date when there was a moment when no one was talking? Suddenly, it felt like it was going to be the worst date ever. We call that the "awkward silence". Have you ever watched the news when an anchor stops talking even for just a few seconds? They call that "dead air". We have created these negative connotations for silence, and yet silence is powerful.

The research by Drs. Michael Bittman of the University of New England and Mark Sipthorp of the Australian Institute of Family Studies argues that "the need for noise and the struggle with silence is a learnt behavior." The filler has become a learned response that we can unlearn by replacing the filler with something more powerful: the pause. The pause is powerful enough to make us seem reflective while allowing us to be calm, cool, and collected.

But the pause is even more powerful than that. It is most powerful...when you can say something...and make your audience...wait...so that they know...that what/you/are about to say....is something....they need...to hear.

Read that last statement again; pause during the ellipses (...) and pause during the slashes (/); if you follow the flow, you just might hear the rhythm. What rhythm do you follow when you speak? Speaking in front of others should be less like a presentation and more like a musical composition. It should have rhythm and flow. That rhythm and flow should be composed...it should be orchestrated...it should be conducted...by your timing, your pacing, and your pausing.

That reminds me of a time when I was standing across the street from a very trendy store that I used to work at when I was in college. As I stood there looking through the store window, I reminisced about how my refusal for help with one particular on-the-job task was actually a formula for using a rhythm to engage others during presentations, conversations, and communications. Years ago, I worked at Urban Outfitters in the Village in New York City. But I wasn't hired to work on the sales floor. And I wasn't hired to ring up customers at the cash register. I was hired to work the bag check area. Customers would come in, put their bags on the counter, and I would give them a number that correlated to a cubby hole on a floor-to-ceiling shelf. I was responsible for giving them a space to leave their belongings while they shopped hands free. For the store, it was a security measure. For me, it was chance to perform...to my own beat. The job was simple...except during the busiest days of the week and the busiest times of the year: Saturdays, the days leading to Christmas, and the back-to-school seasons. There were only so many cubby holes for the parade of customers who loved to visit the store: some to shop, others to buy, many to sightsee. At the height of the continuous stream of people, there were people to the left crowding in and people to the right squeezing out. And me...I was in the middle of it all, scaling the wall like Spiderman; stretching across the space, right foot on a cubby hole, left foot on the counter. My body contorted to hand a satchel to the very cute smile of a blonde-haired tourist from Spain who seemed to be entertained by how my body was rhythmically orchestrated by the tunes dancing through the speakers. Simultaneously and seamlessly, as Marie, a regular at the store, ran in to exchange a skirt she had bought a week prior, I transferred 5 bags from her hands to the cube on the wall. Those were just two people in a blur of bags. And there I was, center stage in front of an audience of customers, tourists, and co-workers. Quite often, to the eyes of my managers, it seemed like it was too much for me to handle.

"Marc, do you need help?", they would ask. Or sometimes, they would not ask; they would just send someone into my little six-foot wide domain. But I would always refuse the help...not because I was too proud to accept the help...but rather because the extra hands would disturb my rhythm. And it was the rhythm that made the performance work. As I stood, perched on the platform, taking and returning bags, I was always performing another task; I was analyzing the flow of the traffic, how many people were coming in versus how many people were leaving; how many bags was one person dropping off and how many bags was another person picking up. It was all about sizing up the number of cubby holes available and the size of the cubby holes necessary to accommodate the bags. It was a very well calculated orchestration...and forget about the days when I would have to create additional space. All those people. All those bags. All those hours. It all was masterminded by the awareness of when to slow down and when to pick up the pace. Side note: There once was a staff member from the David Letterman Show who pitched doing a spot on my performance; unfortunately, the idea never made it to air, but the fact that it was considered makes me proud of my performance. But again, the performance would not have worked without the rhythm. Rhythm is essential to just about everything we do: from driving to exercising, from taking a golf swing to dancing a tango, from eating to communicating, from walking to talking. When you pace strategically, you engage automatically. Rhythm Moves the Crowd.

I read a portion of a syllabus from a class at Yale that shared the following about the power of rhythm and pacing in the delivery of our words: *"Rhythm has a direct access to the unconscious. It can hypnotize the mind and enter our bodies creating a movement. It has a power when it is read. To human beings, rhythm is a natural thing. 'The rhythm of poetry is sometimes said to be based on the rhythm of work, but no one wonders then why we work rhythmically. The heartbeat—pa-thunk, pa-thunk, pa-thunk' (Hass, 1984). Rhythm is all around us, if you listen closely to the sounds surrounding you. It is something we notice at a young age. If you listen right now, you will probably hear a rhythm whether it is the crashing of the waves or the passing of the cars, it is there. Humans find comfort in rhythm. It creates an order, making us feel safe and secure. It helps us predict what will happen next, and it helps us remember what we have just experienced." (Laura Namnoum, yale.edu).* Yes, this is a syllabus for a poetry class, but rhythm is not limited to poetry or music. Rhythm empowers our message and engages our audiences.

So how can you create rhythm and pacing in your delivery to capture the attention and retention of your audience? Follow these three essential steps:

1. Consider how you can break up your sentences. Where would you pause between words? To determine that consider the number of syllables you are using and how you group them together. If this sounds like poetry or the composition of music and lyrics, that's because you should deliver your words like a work of poetry, like a musical composition. I subconsciously do it now, but it begins with a conscious and calculated practice of creating a syllable count or a pattern in your words. This is not necessarily something you would do throughout the entire presentation, but at strategic points where you have a point you want to make stick. We remember jingles, songs, nursery rhymes, and Christmas songs throughout a lifetime and well beyond generations. Using a poetic approach is what will help your message stick.

2. Choose the words you are going to emphasize and accent. Track the distance between those words. How many words or syllables will you emphasize? How far apart are each of those words or syllables from each other? Shakespeare wrote his dialogue in iambic pentameter which actually mimics they way we naturally talk. We naturally accent certain words and syllables. That makes this tip easy to follow. But, if you want to engage your audience, don't just rely on what's natural; instead, depend on what's strategic. Your strategy should be identifying and spacing your words and syllables for emphasis.

3. Always think about how you want your audience to feel: excited, sad, calm, anxious, etc. Those feelings are orchestrated by the pace of your delivery. Why are you speaking so fast? Why are you slowing down when you speak? How do those decisions match the meaning and emotions of your words? Those are good questions to ask, but more importantly those are good prompts to guide your pace and rhythm.

Count your syllables. Create a pattern.

Choose your emphasis. Distance those words.

Consider the desired emotional impact. Adjust your pace.

Standing across the street from Urban Outfitters, I reminisced about how my performance at bag check was like delivering a presentation. I was putting on a show, a one man show. I didn't want help, not because I thought, "I can do it by myself", but rather because I thought, "I'm in a rhythm." Your rhythm is your answer. By the way, there was only one time ever when the manager forced a co-worker to join me and I didn't mind...because together, we were an orchestra...in tune, in pace, in rhythm with each other. It was the only time it worked; any other time the manager tried to put another person in there with me, we would bump into each other, reach for the same bags, and drop items on the floor. It was a mess, a cacophony. We weren't in-sync, so it didn't work. Rhythm works. **So when you prepare your presentation, listen to the way you speak first.** If you hear the rhythm when you speak, you'll be ready to move the crowd. And then just like your listeners' favorite songs, they will stay tuned into you. When you create your flow, your audience will follow. It's all in the pacing, the pausing, and the timing.

Part Three:
The Expansion of Engagement

Chapter 16:
Answering a Few Questions

I've been very fortunate to have the privilege of teaching my Rules of Engagement class to a wide variety of learners and listeners. And whenever there is an opportunity to teach beyond the rules, I welcome it. So I would like to dedicate this chapter to those who have posed questions during a workshop to deepen their understanding and mastery of the rules.

How do you stand with a disability?

It's not about how you stand. Rather, it's about not moving around too much. We see a lot of people walk all around the stage or back and forth in front of the room. It's either because they are nervous or because they did not intentionally plan to move with purpose. As I've said before, the Common Denominator of Success is Preparation. So the answer to that question really is: You want to think about it BEFORE you come up in front of the room: where you want to stand and why you want to stand there. If you were to take a look at my "Short on Confidence" speech, you would see that I started on the right side of the stage (at my starting line). And then there was a point when I talked about how I was afraid to do something (so I backed up, because that's what we tend to do when we are afraid of something). And then I said, "I'm about to do something I never thought I'd ever do in public. But I'm going to do it." Then I stepped forward and walked towards the front of the stage (as we often do when we are ready to confidently confront something). And then each time I told another part of the story, I moved to my left. By the end of the speech, I went from my starting line (my extended right), where I WAS that kid who was afraid to wear shorts, to my finish line (my extended left), where I BECAME that person who was happy to compete in the International Speech Contest "in my shorts". So it's not about any disability, but rather it's about the ability to determine how you will stand, where and when you will stand, and how you will move with purpose.

What would you say is the best way to deal with self-consciousness? For example, I'm tall, and I like the fact that I'm tall. But sometimes though, when I'm feeling awkward, it feels as though I'm going to stand out too much for being tall. And I feel like I have to restrict my movement because I don't have the greatest flexibility. How do I best prevent that from getting in the way of my message?

So you actually answered your question without even realizing it. It's the MESSAGE. One problem that most people have with public speaking is SELF-consciousness or SELF-judgment. What are people thinking when they are looking at us? Are they judging us or criticizing us? When I take my attention off of myself and focus on the MESSAGE, then at the end of the day I don't care if I'm tall or skinny, standing with my pants down or my shorts on; I just want you to walk away with a MESSAGE. If you focus on the MESSAGE that you want THEM to receive, then your message-for-their-benefit has the power to take away from your SELF-consciousness.

Do you get bored with the speech? You said you were working on the speech [Short on Confidence] for eight months. Was there a point when you couldn't stand to give it anymore?

The answer to that is "No" and I'll tell you why. I remember competing a couple of years ago when I advanced to the third round. I felt like I was getting bored with the speech. So the following year when I competed, I came up with this "brilliant" idea: Every round, should I advance, I was going to deliver a different speech. That didn't work out. I advanced no further than I had the previous contest season. Furthermore, it didn't allow me to revise my message to progression, not perfection, but progression. Everything has room for improvement. What worked for me was what I did in 2014. If you were to look at the evolution of the "Short on Confidence" speech, even when I delivered it at a Toastmasters Conference three months after competing for the World Championship, you would see that it was a different speech than when I delivered it in Malaysia, which was different than when I delivered it at the District 46 Conference before Malaysia, which was different than when I did it in the third, second, and even the first round. That's because I received a lot of feedback along the way and I took it in and made adjustments. Your message is most powerful when it lives in constant revision. So even when it comes to my Rules of Engagement seminar, the way that I open it now is different than how I opened it when I first delivered it in front of an audience. If you have a particular presentation that you want to deliver on a lot of different occasions, revise it and change it around; make it new and fresh for you.

You mentioned that when preparing, you speak it out, then record it, and then you write it down. But that might be difficult for non-native speakers who may find that challenging. Do you have any suggestions for them?

I would say the same thing I told students in my classes. Sit down and brainstorm, just like we would do in an English class, and jot things down. It is important to write down some brief notes immediately after you start coming up with ideas because a lot of times, we keep those thoughts in our heads, and then two or three days later, or even two or three hours later, it doesn't come out the way we wanted it to. So it is very important, whether it's much later like in my process or earlier in your process, to write everything down. I now carry a small notebook with me everywhere I go to jot down my thoughts. And when I can't access that, I pull out my phone and draft some notes in an email that I send to myself. I recommend that everyone else do the same: log your thoughts, your experiences, your observations, your ideas, your stories, etc. If it's difficult to do that because you are a non-native speaker, then write it in your native tongue. You can always translate it later. The preservation of an idea is more crucial than the words you can translate or proofread later.

Another participant added that instead of writing down her speech, she records bits and pieces of it as she composes it.

I responded that I started doing that as well. Recording myself takes less time than writing down my thoughts. And often, it's more convenient because we tend to have a phone in reach more often than we have a pen or pencil in hand. Furthermore, there are now apps you can use to then transcribe the audio recording of your voice. I recommend this practice because a lot of times I, like other people, will have these ideas floating around in my head that I don't want to lose. If I don't have my little notebook, I can use the recorder on my phone to safekeep those ideas.

You talked about preparation; being prepared; don't memorize; and having confidence. Would you share with us...you said for every minute of a speech, you need an hour...so to do this tonight, how long did you prepare? And listening to you and engaging with you, because you are making eye contact, it looks like we're having a conversation sitting at a table together and not that this is a presentation. So how is all that accomplished?

Here are a few things: I prepare by using a method that I used to be hesitant to recommend. Now I suggest it all the time. I call it the Jay-Z/Lil' Wayne Method. Upon watching several documentaries, I remember learning that the two famous hip-hop artists, Jay-Z and Lil' Wayne, don't actually write down their lyrics when they are composing. They go into a studio and they just "jam". And then after they create the song, they write down the lyrics. The "writing it down afterwards" was the part I did not do for a long time, and as a result, I lost a lot of speeches that I loved. I've learned my lesson since then. Now I record my presentations and then transcribe them afterwards. But I compose my presentations through a "jam session" first. And I like doing it that way because it is the most organic way to create your unique voice, the one that resembles the way you naturally speak in a conversation. It's less about the mechanics of writing a speech and trying to get the perfect words, and more about creating a talk in your own language and in your own voice. And that's why I'm happy to hear that you feel like my talk *sounds like a conversation, because my goal is not to sound like anybody else; I'm talking like me.*

The second part is the preparation. And I will tell you: there was a time after my wife and I had dropped our kids off at camp, before I left for Malaysia, when my wife said, "Are you talking about that speech again?" We were shopping for groceries and I had this idea. And she said, "Oh my God. You are not talking about that speech again." One night, we were watching "Keeping Up with the Kardashians" because she likes the Kardashians-Okay, maybe I like them too, (but that's besides the point), and during a commercial break, I said, "Wait, I got this idea..." She interrupted me, "Are you talking about that speech again?"

I was. I was talking about it again and again. I was thinking about it again and again. I was practicing it again and again. I become married to my speech. When I get up in the morning, and when I'm getting ready for work, I will go through at least a part of a speech. When I walk to work, or if I go for a walk around the park, I will go through the speech in my head. If I have a break at work, I'll go over the speech. I'm always going through it in my head, while picturing where I'm standing and how I'm gesturing. (I envision how I want to deliver it; and that's how you have to see it, as a vision, not just a set of words to be spoken, but as a vision that will be experienced). Then at night, when I'm at home, and everyone has gone to sleep, I will stand in front of the muted-TV-because the TV is my simulated audience-and I will then go through the motions. You have to be that committed to your preparation. You have to be that committed to your listeners.

How long should you maintain eye contact during an interview?

You should maintain eye contact throughout the duration of an interview. Remember, making eye contact doesn't mean you're staring down nor creeping out the other person. It shows that you are attentive when being spoken to and that you are confident when you are speaking. You can break eye contact for a brief moment after the interviewer completes the question and before you begin answering.

During that short span of time, you can break eye contact to show that you are thinking of a solid response.

How do you speak for a long period of time without some kind of audience question/engagement, if you are used to that kind of interaction?

Audience interaction is golden because after all, you are speaking for their value, not for your accolades. There is no rule that you have to speak for 10, 15, 30, nor 60 straight minutes. Plan your talk in a way that breaks up your monologue with moments for questions, however often you feel comfortable. There have been times when I have delivered my training session of the ten rules, and I would take questions after every two rules. So create those breaks in your talks. As Darren Lacroix once said to me: "You are the CEO of your talk." You can design it the way you see fit, and the way that fits your comfort.

If my goal is to use vocal variety, what advice would you give about using different tones?

"Tone is not the word you are looking for. Emotions is the key word." Ask yourself what 2-3 emotions you want people to feel when you are speaking. Speak with those emotions. Then, use your facial expressions to mirror those emotions. And when you can, add dialogue from the instance you are talking about because when we imitate people's voices, we tend to change our voices. Emotions and dialogue are the keys to sounding more expressive when you speak.

Sometimes I have trouble remembering what I had planned to say. What do you recommend I do to remember my thoughts without memorizing every word?

To reduce the chances of forgetting your talking points, as you prepare for the presentation, break them up into small soundbites of 1-2 minutes. Then give each soundbite a six-word title. On the days leading up to the presentation, spend 1-2 minute intervals throughout the day to practice each soundbite. This can help you to internalize your message in manageable chunks.

Chapter 17:
An Extension of the Rules

From time to time, I have taken to the internet to publish tips designed to give you the power to make others pay attention to you when you speak. Consider these an extension of the Rules of E.N.G.A.G.E.M.E.N.T.

Change Your Mood

What's that voice in your head? And why should you listen to it?

As I sat in the catering hall and listened to a host of talented speakers, I was trying my hardest to listen to them, but it was a challenge because there was this voice in my head...it was Britney Spears singing about a "Circus".

Minutes before that moment, which was an hour before I was scheduled to speak, I had stepped outside and walked around the parking lot. Every once in a while, I would stop to practice my speech. And then, I started walking again...well, it was less like a walk, and more like a two-step...Yes, I was stepping to the music. I was "getting down". There was a "party" going on in my head. And I could not contain myself. My earplugs were charging my brain. The noise was feeding me energy. The music was altering my mood. I was in a trance that took me back to the third grade.

"When I was in elementary school, our teachers organized a cultural assembly. I was a part of the African dancers segment. I felt self-conscious, as we danced down the aisle of the auditorium, shirt-less, wearing very short shorts covered by grass belts cut out of construction paper. Nevertheless, when we got to the stage, we performed a number in unison before breaking out into solo moves. I never expected to be a solo dancer, but during a rehearsal, the teacher in charge, who I believe was trying her best to help me build my self-esteem and self-confidence, asked me to dance to the music by myself. After some trepidation, I broke out a few steps that ended with this backwards snake-like move I saw in Michael Jackson's "Beat It" video. And that was all she needed to see. I don't think the moves were spectacular. But I think my shell cracked at that moment. It was a breakthrough. And I have music to thank for it." **(an excerpt from my book Beyond Limitations)**.

After I danced around the parking lot to the rhythm of Brittany Spears' "Circus", I was in a zone. My mood had changed. Yes, I was still nervous about speaking in front of all those people, but the music relaxed me and it allowed me to do something that everyone should do anytime you stand before a crowd to say a few words (have fun). The music put me in a good mood and allowed me to have fun!

We have to have fun when we are speaking. It's paramount to our ability to keep the audience engaged. Fun is contagious. Energy is contagious. And Music is a source of fun and energy.

So what is that voice in your head that is singing a tune that puts you in a fun mood? Make sure you listen to it before you speak. Athletes do it. Artists do it. Even President Obama had a playlist for his inauguration.

Rule of Engagement: When you charge your brain with your favorite tune, you can change the mood of the entire room.

When Eye Smile

If adults only smile 20 times a day, then how likely is it that we are not smiling while we are speaking in front of an audience? Do you smile when you are delivering a presentation? If so, how often do you smile while you're talking? And if not, why not? I once caught myself nearly regretting putting a smile on my face.

I was standing by my car, waiting for my family to return from the zoo. As I read an article, preparing for a talk I was booked to deliver, I noticed yet another person walking by. As usual, I looked up, made eye contact, nodded, and smiled. As the gentleman in the jogging suit continued to walk by, he glanced back at me. I nodded and smiled again. A few steps later, he glanced again. I nodded and smiled again. This all happened within 10-15 steps of him walking by. Then he stopped, pierced his eyes into mine, and said, "Why are you smiling?"

I could feel the tension.

All of a sudden, what I've always believed to be a friendly gesture seemed to have become a weapon. In some way, I was violating him. His serious expression demanded an answer.

"Because I'm happy," I replied.

Then I continued, "I'm always happy. We should all be happy. If we're not happy, then something is wrong in the world. That's why I smile and make eye contact. Too many people walk around with their heads down, avoiding eye contact and not smiling at others. That's not working for us. That's why I smile and make eye contact."

There was a moment of stillness.

Then he looked at me and replied...with a smile, "Alright." And then he continued his walk.

That morning, I had to explain why I smile because the human connection has become threatening. The smile has become a weapon. Eye contact has become a dagger. Or maybe it's not that extreme.

Maybe it's simply that smiling has become too laborious, too invasive, too fake.

After that brief moment, I continued to wait for my family to return. Meanwhile, tens of people walked by. Only one made eye contact, nodded, and smiled. Then a young woman in shades strolled into my peripheral vision. I looked up and nodded. She returned the smile and mouthed the words "Good morning". Then, a father followed his two boys who were too caught up in their game to notice me. But their dad noticed my nod and smile. He returned the nod, but not the smile. And then some of the park workers started to come out. One stood inches from me. I looked up. She wouldn't even look up as she picked up a piece of trash near my foot. I wish she would have looked up and smiled. I wish everyone would just smile more often. It would make us all feel better.

I'm reminded of my Aunt Grace. May God rest her soul and use her smile to shine upon our world. When I was a kid, I used to visit her at work. Sometimes, we would take walks. And I always noticed that she said hello to and smiled at almost everyone. I used to think it was so cool that my aunt Grace knew so many people. But as I grew older, I realized that she didn't know most of those people. She was just that friendly.

We need to be more friendly. We need to make eye contact more often. We need to nod more often. We need to smile more often. We need to acknowledge and welcome each other's presence more often. We need to be happy more often. Smiling is not a weapon. Smiling is a cure for the many ills we often face in society.

Researchers who study smiling have found that a smile:

. is contagious

. lowers stress and anxiety

. makes us more attractive

. releases endorphins

. strengthens our immune system

. makes us more approachable

. makes us more comfortable

. makes us seem more trustworthy

. and makes us better leaders

I realize that smiling at strangers can sometimes be awkward or maybe even threatening, but the outcomes are so much more rewarding. When we speak in front of an audience, we are more often than not standing before a room of strangers. That makes it difficult to think about smiling. But we should smile.

An article in Psychology Today explained that some of the reasons why we don't smile at strangers (and keep in mind that when we deliver presentations, we're often nervous because we are speaking to a room full of strangers) are because 1) our minds are preoccupied with other thoughts (like thinking of what to say while we're speaking), 2) it's tough to muster up a genuine smile (if public speaking is one of the top fears in the world, then most people might find it extremely difficult to feel like smiling at that moment), and 3) smiling often invites people into a world that we don't want them in (most people are afraid to speak in public because they're afraid of being judged or being exposed; they're uncomfortable with the attention). In essence, the last thing on our minds when we find ourselves speaking in front of an audience of strangers is to remember to smile.

But I encourage you all to remind yourselves to smile. It will make you feel better. It will make them feel better. It will create a positive experience for us all.

Rule of Engagement: When you speak with a smile, you invite the room to relax, enjoy, and listen for a while.

End in Mind

Spoiler Alert: Here's how the story ends; he did not get the job. But he learned an important lesson about how to communicate when you want to get hired.

As I sat in a friendly neighborhood Starbucks, I overheard this interview question, "So what would you do if a member of your team was not performing up to par, hindering the success of the team, and refusing to change?" The interviewee did exactly what many people have been taught about interviewing, public speaking, and communicating in general: "Always respond with a story." So he told his story with rich details that gave a clear picture of his leadership style. Then after a few follow-up questions, he gave the answer that the interviewers were looking to hear. "I fired the guy." One of the interviewers said, "That's what I was waiting to hear. Why didn't you say that at first?" Then she gave this advice to the interviewee: "During an interview, think about what answer the interviewer is looking for, cut to the chase and give that answer, and then fill in the details of the story afterwards."

Now that may be true for an interview because time is of the essence and your audience may not have the time nor patience for a story, but how true is that for a prepared speech or presentation? Very. But not because time is of the essence but rather because curiosity makes people pay attention. When your audience is curious to hear more, you have achieved exactly what every speaker desires.

But haven't we all been told that the best way to engage an audience is with a story. Toastmasters have heard it: "Tell a story. Make a point." And research proves it: Stories light up multiple parts of the brain. So why would anyone want to give away the ending and give up the chance to engage the audience? They shouldn't. I'm not suggesting that we forego telling stories. That would be detrimental and dry to our speech. What I am suggesting is an unconventional or at least a rarely used rule of engagement. Before you tell a story, tell the ending.

The ending will make your audience curious about the details in the middle. I remember reading an article about why we are scientifically engaged by stories; it's because we are naturally curious about "cause and effect". So when we tell someone about the effect, they are curious about the cause. That reminds me about the formula for making sales (after all, aren't we all "selling" an idea or a message?). The formula is Then-Now-How. Tell them first what the condition was at the beginning: *Then*; tell them what is happening currently: *Now*; tell them the solution: *How* you will get them from their *Then* to what could be their *Now*. Notice that the *How* comes last because after you peak the interest of the audience with the *Then* and the *Now*, they will want to know more about the *How*. The *How* is the story; everyone wants to hear a story. They just need an incentive to listen. And that incentive is the ending of the story. Tell them the *Then-and-Now* now and they will want to hear the *How* later.

Spoiler update: So the truth is, I have no way of truly knowing whether or not the guy got the job. But I do know that he learned a valuable lesson as did I. The goal every time we speak is to get the audience so engaged that they are asking for more. So the next time, you want to make a point with a story, try something different.

Rule of Engagement: When you start with the end of the tale, you'll make them curious about what else you have to tell.

Ask and You Shall Tell

Here's a question to ask yourself: How do you tell a story that will wow a crowd? From the campfire to the classroom to the corporate office, when we communicate, we often use stories to make our point. Why? Because stories are fascinating. Because stories are memorable. Because stories work.

Brain research shows that stories tend to light up multiple parts of the brain, making our listeners more alert and more engaged. That explains why we often hear the phrase: Tell a story. Make a point. But one of the most challenging things to do as a communicator is to create a story that works...that is until you learn to ask a question...But before I share with you what to ask, here's a story.

As my son sat down at the kitchen table to do his homework, he was stuck. He didn't know how to start or where to start. It was a classic case of writer's block. Have you ever had a case of writer's block? If you've ever had to deliver a presentation, sell with a conversation, prepare for an interview, or create a story for a homework assignment, then you've experienced writer's block?

So what have you done to "unblock"? Writer's block is often associated with creating stories. And that's exactly what my son had to do for homework. His teacher told him to write a story about a cold place.

Ten minutes passed.

Five more minutes passed.

He dropped his head on the table in pure frustration.

The pencil fell to the floor.

He thought he would never be able to do it, until I asked him...

But before I tell you what I asked...I would like to share that I'm glad his teacher assigned that task because it teaches a very important skill that we all can use to engage our listeners: storytelling. So how do you tell a story that engages? I'm glad you asked...

When I was in Kuala Lumpur, Malaysia, competing for the World Championship of Public Speaking, I learned so many valuable lessons about storytelling. And many of those lessons are driven by questions we can ask ourselves to "unblock" in order to engage.

Ask yourself: In this story, what is the message that I am trying to convey? Then answer that question in 10-12 words. A concise statement will give you the clarity you need to craft a story that will engage.

Ask yourself: When or how did you learn that lesson or information? The occasion when you learned the lesson/message/information is the story you may be looking for to wow your audience.

Ask yourself: How do you then craft that story? I have the answer my friends.

Admittedly, I was never the best storyteller. I remember conversations with one of my closest friends. I would ramble on while he would captivate. I am always mesmerized by him because he has such a knack for storytelling. He might be one of the best storytelling conversationalists I've ever met. A storytelling conversationalist by the way is a term I created to describe anyone who weaves stories into their conversations. We can all be storytelling conversationalist; we just have to know the questions to ask before we tell the story.

My friend is so good at telling stories because he never tells a story without the purpose of making a point. He understands how important that is. But he's also good at it because everyone of his stories answers the questions...Once you know the questions to ask, you can create a story for any occasion. Without those questions, some people, myself included, have found that they rarely told stories; instead we only shared situations. What's missing from the unfinished situation that could make it an engaging story? The answers to the questions...

But before I share those questions...(Oh no, am I really going to make you wait longer...yes...but the answer is closer than you think.)

Let's get some clarity on the difference between a situation and a story. The situation my son had to write about was about a person who lives in a cold place. Situation: "There was this teacher at my school who used to live in Wisconsin, which is a very cold place. She used to sleep in three layers of clothes under a thick blanket by her portable heater. I'm never moving to Wisconsin." Let's turn this situation into a story by asking four essential questions: Who? What? Why not? and How?

Anytime you find yourself in a conversation, presentation, or interview and you choose to use a story to engage your listener, ask yourself these four questions before you start:

1. Who is the story about?
2. What is the person trying to do?
3. Why can't that person do it?
4. How does the person do it?

When my son hit that writer's block, those were the questions I asked him to unblock and engage. I don't have a copy of what he wrote, but my version would go like this: "My teacher used to live in Wisconsin in an extremely cold apartment. She tried to get her landlord to fix the heat, but he never answered her phone calls. So after one more night of sleeping in three layers of clothes, underneath a very thick blanket, next to the portable heater, she called the mayor's office and filed a complaint about her landlord. Later that day, the landlord sent in someone to fix the heat for the entire building. If someone doesn't answer your call for help, then call someone else to help that person to help you."

So what's the difference between the situation and the story: the conflict, the means by which it is resolved, and the purpose of sharing the story. Those are the elements that make stories compelling and those are the elements that are crafted through the answers to those questions. Ask those questions and you shall tell.

Stories are the best way to get your point across, but we often find ourselves blocked by the process of creativity. So when you want to unblock and engage, follow an actual process.

1. Determine your purpose.
2. Select from memory the moment you learned the information yourself.
3. Ask and Answer Who?, What?, Why not? And how?
4. Compose your story and share it.

Or simply put: Ask and You Shall Tell.

Rules of Engagement: If you want to tell a story that makes the crowd go "wow", craft your story with these four questions, Who?, What?, Why not?, and How?

Surprise! Surprise! Surprise!

I never saw it coming and neither should they...Not if you want it to work.

When I dropped my kids off to school one morning, I had a feeling that the day was going to be a little different. The kids lined up in the school yard as usual, but the teachers arrived a little bit earlier. The principal positioned herself in the center of the yard, not in the lobby this time as usual. And off to the corner, far from the classroom where he usually preps in the morning, the music teacher checked the microphone, "Check 1. Check 2. Check 3." Parents glanced at each other with questions marked on our faces.

The principal paused for silence. She glanced at the small children standing at attention. Then she flashed a smile to the parents. All of sudden, a burst of, "3, 2, 1!" danced through the air. And through the side doors of the school building, marched a jubilant jazz band. Chanting. Playing. Dancing. Smiling.

Surprise! Surprise! Surprise! What a way to start the day!

A father two-stepped and wiggled his hips to the beat. A mother tapped her fingers across the fence to the rhythm of the drumsticks. Two small children sprang to their feet and twirled each other around to the chorus of smaller clapping hands. A wave of teachers accompanied the principal as she paraded the parents into the yard for the party. And what made it even better is that this occurred in the school yard, which means that it wasn't just a celebration for the kids. And it wasn't just a celebration for the parents. It was also a celebration for the entire community!

Surprise! Surprise! Surprise! What a way to start the day!

It was unlike every other day we had seen! It was something different, which is why we won't forget it. And it made us look forward to the rest of the day. And that's the goal!

Imagine:

If only every school day could start that way.

If only every work day could start that way.

If only every day could start that way!

But then it wouldn't work, would it? The way we get things started has a profound impact on that which follows. But when it gets started differently than before, it has an even greater effect!

We should remember that not only every morning, but also every time we stand before an audience to speak. How do you start what you say? What do you do differently at the beginning of your presentations? Here's an idea:

Do the unexpected. If they never see what's coming, they're more likely to look forward to what will follow.

Now I'm not suggesting that we start our talks with marching bands, choral numbers, or dance ensembles, because it's not the big band that works. What works is the big surprise! Joel Olsteen starts his sermons with humorous anecdotes. And those stories work because the endings are unanticipated. The endings are funny and we never see them coming. Surprise! Surprise! Surprise! What a way to start what he has to say!

Mohammed Qahtani began his 2015 World Championship speech by lighting a cigarette and sharing some alarming statistics about smokers. Surprise! Then he confessed that he lied about the numbers just to prove how powerful words can be. No one saw that coming. He surprised us and then he surprised us again. Surprise! Surprise! Surprise! What a way to start what he had to say!

But on the flipside, when I stepped on stage to compete in the finals of the 2014 International Speech Contest, I began by leading the auditorium in a song. It was awful! The moment I said, "I was listening to this song the other day", the audience could see it coming, but they so badly wanted it to go away...not the song, but my singing. Oh yeah, it was unbearable and unwelcomed. Have you ever received a gift you wanted to give back? That's my voice. But it wasn't really the bad singing that didn't work. It was the fact that there's nothing unusual about singing to people, even when the singing is good.

There's nothing surprising about something common. The Same. The Same. The Lame. Did I lose the audience? No. The rest of the speech was received well. But I lost the competition, and I believe that outcome was due to the way I began the speech. It wasn't a bad start. It just wasn't unique. What a usual way to start what I had to say!

So what did I learn from two accomplished speakers, from the principal at my kids' school, and from my mishap on stage?

The best way to start what you say is by doing something unexpected to get the audience connected. Brain research shows that the pleasure center of the brain lights up like a Christmas tree when we are exposed to the unexpected. *"Scientists using magnetic resonance imaging (MRI) to measure brain activity in response to pleasurable stimuli found that the nucleus accumbens — a region known as the brain's pleasure center — responded much more strongly when the event was unanticipated (Julia Sommerfeld, MSNBC).* By the way, the research concluded that the effect is the same whether it is a happy surprise or a not-so-happy surprise. The impact is created less by the emotion and more by the surprise.

So the next time you are preparing a presentation, ask yourself, what can I say or do at the beginning that they will not see coming? And then deliver your surprise.

There are so many hooking strategies out there that you can use to start your speech. And you should read about all of them so you can expand the tools you can use when you follow the "rules". But remember: the key to making any of them work is the element of surprise. When they don't see it coming, they are more likely to follow.

Rule of Engagement: If you want to them to connect, start with something they won't expect.

P.S. There's a speech where the guy started by pulling down his pants? He was inspired by watching a former world champion of public speaking who started his speech by falling on his face and staying down. What a way to start what they had to say. And both of those beginnings worked because no one ever saw them coming! And even though, at first sight, both seemed like cheap ploys to grab the attention of the audience, when you see both speeches in their entirety, you will see how those openings connected with the overall message. As a matter of fact, neither speech would have worked without those unique starters (if I may say so myself, considering that I was the one who delivered that speech "in my shorts"!)

Surprise! Surprise! Surprise!

In Just One Hour

Question: How much time do you need to say what's on your mind?

Answer: At least one hour.

But don't worry. It won't take an hour for you to read what I've prepared to say. And it shouldn't take an hour for it to sink in. But if you want to engage your audience every time you stand before a crowd to say a few words, then you will want to take at least one hour to apply this rule. So are you ready? No really, are you ready? I can't tell you how many times I've been asked that question.

And yet, I found myself at a networking event in a lounge one night when all of the people in attendance were given the opportunity to speak for 1-2 minutes about what we do. There were nearly 100 of us squooshed in the basement of an uptown bar. The lights were barely strong enough to see the faces in the room. The blaring rhythms of disco music drowned out the many voices that confessed, "I don't even know what to say." Nights before, when I was invited, a friend shared, "This will be a great opportunity for you to tell people about *what you do.*" I knew what I was in for, but I didn't prepare. And that explains why my five-minute elevator pitch was a babbling disaster.

I wasn't ready. I hadn't practiced. I didn't invest my one hour. How much time do you invest? When you know you have to deliver a talk, go on an interview, present a case, or run a meeting, how much time do you spend practicing?

It's one thing to prepare your message (and that is critically important), but practicing the delivery of your message is equally important. You don't have to be perfect, but you have to be practiced. If you want to engage your audience, you have to be prepared for that moment. If you want to perform your best, you have to take the time to prepare. Nothing great has ever been accomplished without preparing for the moment. No great athlete accomplishes anything great without lots of practice: *"Most marathon training plans range from 12 to 20 weeks leading up to race day." (Tyler Tervooren).* No great performer accomplishes anything great without lots of practice: *"A typical Broadway show rehearses six days a week for eight hours a day. The company then moves to the theatre for tech rehearsal — which can last one-and-a-half to two weeks for a big musical — where the hours get longer." (Zachary Pincus-Roth).* No great musician accomplishes anything great without lots of practice: *"No matter who you are, you need to rehearse a lot to build up your muscle memory of what works so you don't even think about how to move, or where to set up and how to read an audience at the end of each song. It has to become second nature. Being on stage has to fit you like a suit, and that happens only by rehearsal."* (Keith Hatschek).

And while you can deliver a very good presentation with little to no practice (or at least a few people can), why settle for being just good, when you can be truly great? If you want to be the kind of speaker who leaves a greater impression on an audience that hangs on your every word, then remember: no effective communicator accomplishes anything amazing on stage without lots of practice off stage: "Dr. Jill Bolte-Taylor rehearsed her TED talk 200 times. It's been viewed 15 million times and Oprah invited her to be a guest on her show. Dr. Jill's TED talk transformed her career." (Carmine Gallo).

200 times? For an 18 minute speech, that's approximately 67 hours of practice, almost four hours for every minute of the speech. That's a lot of time. That's what it takes to be greater. Look at the results. But if you're not aiming for Oprah numbers, that's fine. But you should be aiming for the number of people in your audience and focusing on being great for them! And to be great for them, it takes at least one hour...one hour for every minute of your presentation, approximately 60 times to practice your talk.

Next time, you have an important talk to deliver, create a log so you can track the time you invest to be your best. And practice, practice, practice. Keep a count of how many times you invest. And practice, practice, practice. Remember, your performance is only as great as your preparation. So be prepared!

Rule of Engagement: If you want your audience to be engaged, spend more time practicing off stage.

P.S. Did anyone hear the babbling monologue of Kanye West at the 2015 MTV Video Music Awards? He had such an opportunity to deliver as strong as he sells records. And unlike other artists who were not sure if they were going to win an award that night, he knew for sure that he would be honored and that he would be expected to address the crowd. It was a grand opportunity to deliver. It was also an essential obligation to be prepared for the moment. And while some might blame it on the alcohol, the truth is, his now infamous 13-minute ramble was impaired by a lack of practice. He could have created a greater moment. And in the bar that night at the networking party, I could have created a greater moment too. But my babble was impaired by a lack of practice. Never again.

Don't be impaired. Be prepared.

Take the time to practice what you want to say:

(one hour of practice for every minute of talk).

And replay it before you say it!

When You Talk Too Much

For how long can you speak without coming up for air?

On two different occasions one week, with two different audiences, and with two different presenters, I overheard someone in the crowd whisper, "He talks too much." Song cue from RunDMC: *"You talk too much and you never shut up."* I hope you never have that problem. But what exactly is the problem with talking too much? The answer may not surprise you.

I watched Chris Rock talk for 60 straight minutes during a comedy routine. I watched Jeffrey Gittomer, sales expert, talk for 120 minutes with just a ten-minute break in between. I heard Barack Obama talk for 45 straight minutes at the 2016 Democratic National Convention. These three, among others, are great speakers, and their long talks didn't lose their audiences. And they have something in common with you. No, they don't talk too much, and neither do you. Like you, many great speakers and leaders just have a lot to say. The problem isn't talking too much; the problem is continuing to talk when you've run out of things to say. The difference between engaging talkers and the two presenters I saw that week is "riveting versus rambling". These two presenters rambled and detoured onto tangents. Don't get caught rambling and detouring.

If you don't want to lose your listeners, follow these two steps:

1. Summarize your purpose and outline your talking points <u>before you speak</u>.
2. Select your own time limit and hold yourself to it.

Rule of Engagement: Economize the words you speak to maximize the attention you get.

Outline in Your Mind

How do you get your words to flow when you speak?

As he walked back to his seat, members of the audience greeted him with high fives, handshakes, and smiles. What an amazing job he did with his presentation. The thing that made it work so well was his structure. His ideas were so easy to follow because he so clearly outlined his points. It was a roadmap for engagement. Think before you talk. Collect your thoughts before you speak. Outline in your mind before you present. Some of the most fluent talkers, from customer service reps to political figures, from celebrity athletes to sweet talkers at the nightclub, are so good at what they do because they formulate a talking plan in their heads before they speak.

Rule of Engagement: Create an outline in your mind of what you want to say before you even say it.

No More Distractions

While he was looking underneath the table at my feet, Jerome noticed that I was doing the side-to-side step throughout the entire presentation. As engaging as the message might have been, the shuffle was too much of a distraction. What do you do with your body when you are speaking in front of other people? For most people, the answer might be "I don't know." or "I've never noticed." Those are the responses that now outline your next step: Become aware. What is your unintentional habit when speaking to others? Become aware of it to fix it. That will help others to fix their attention on you.

Rule of Engagement: If you want people to pay attention to you, pick one distracting habit that you will no longer do.

When You Lean

As he stood near the foot of the stage to address the crowd, he leaned back, resting his back, arms, and shoulders against the wall. What was he trying to communicate through his posture? Was he even aware of his posture? More importantly, did he give any thought about his posture before he spoke?

When you speak to people, do you give thought to the way you posture your body as it connects to the message you want to convey and the outcome you desire from that conversation? If so, great! If not, start giving it some thought. Research shows that when we lean in, we communicate that we are attentive; when we lean over, we communicate control, superiority, or aggressiveness; when we lean back, we may communicate comfort, but then again, we might be communicating a cavalier or arrogant attitude. When we stand or sit straight, we might communicate formality, equality, or rigidity. Posture is a complicated issue.

So how should you posture yourself when you speak? The answer is not in the body, but in the intent. Think about what your intended outcome is and then posture your body to communicate the message you want to deliver.

Rule of Engagement: To get the desired result from a conversation or presentation, be intentional about the language you want your posture to speak.

Metaphorically Speaking

Have you ever tried to explain something that was difficult to understand? What metaphor did you use to illustrate your point? The metaphor is a powerful tool because it gives you the opportunity to say what you want to say in the most unique way. And why is that so important...because people will not just pay attention to you, but also, they will remember you when you say it in a way they will never forget.

Dr. Oliver T. Reid, motivational speaker, shared that when he was a little boy, his mother reached into the depths of the freezer to pull out a frozen pack of expired meat. "After this thaws out," she said, "this will be the best meal you will ever have." And it was. Dr. Reid then dropped this one on us....our dreams may be frozen, but they have not expired. Let those dreams thaw out so you can see what amazing achievements you can still cook up in your life. He left me with a metaphor I'll never forget. I left the room inspired to complete a mission to do something unforgettable. Just you wait until it thaws out.

What metaphor will you deliver to keep your listeners tuned into you long after you have spoken?

Rule of Engagement: Use a metaphor to paint a picture that will never leave their minds.

The Sound of Your Speak

How do you sound when you speak? It was 2:00 AM when I was watching a doctor being interviewed on a show about the problem with taking daily supplements. What stood out to me was the tone of the interviewee's voice. If she could have heard herself speak, she would have noticed that her voice was very robotic; very monotonous; very automated. The sound of her voice reminded me of what I hear when someone is reading to an audience or when a salesperson is dragging on and on through the same script he's been delivering during cold calls all day long. She sounded like she wasn't excited about what she was saying.

How often are you excited about what you are saying? Tone can be a product of how tired you are with a message, or how routine the delivery of the message has become. So how do you add life to your message so that you can add life to the sound of your voice? Switch the order of your talking points. Trade in your old story for a new one. Replace some of your vocabulary. Don't just revise your message, but revamp the way you say it to keep it fresh and exciting for you.

Rule of Engagement: When you revamp your message, you can revitalize your delivery.

When your voice sounds excited, your listeners will feel excited. And that is how you can get the results you want when you speak.

Chapter 18:
Bringing It to a Close

Waiting for my flight home from Malaysia, I had my earphones plugged into an educational CD by Darren Lacroix called "Get Paid to Speak in a Week". Before he got into the tips, he posed an important question: Why? What are your why's? I've extended that question to: What or Who are the reasons why you do what you do? We all have reasons: reasons to be better speakers, better listeners, better leaders, better people, better versions of our future selves. My greatest reason is my wife and kids. My family is the reason why I do what I do: My wife Lauren and my children; Jordan, Sydney, and Dylan. But I have another reason. That reason is you. Helping you drives me.

I want to give you the power to make others pay attention to you when you speak. I want to give you the world and everything beyond it. And I'm willing to stay up late working on this passion. And I'm willing to study books, videos, and audios in addition to my other professional responsibilities. And I'm willing to travel the world to touch and improve your life and the lives of many others. But the hardest part of what I love to do is that I won't always be able to bring my family (my greatest reason) with me when I travel to speak, whether it be for international, national, or even local talks.

It was hard for me to go to Malaysia without my family for so long. It's even difficult to leave them for short trips. I remember one year when I was competing in a Humorous Speech Contest. As I walked out of my house, my little Sydney started to cry. It broke my heart.

"What's wrong Sydney? You don't want daddy to leave?"

She shook her head with her lips curled upside down.

"But what if I bring home a trophy?"

Her face rose, her lips lifted, and her head nodded joyfully.

So then I went to the Humorous Speech Contest and I made my best attempt at making the audience listen and laugh...but at the end of the night, I came in second place. It was disappointing, but not entirely...because second place...gets a trophy!

I brought that trophy home and showed it to my little girl and she smiled from ear to ear! That made me happy...not just because I made my little girl smile, but also because I set two examples for my little girl and my two little boys:

1) Set a Goal. Pursue a Dream.

2) Your Voice is your Power. Your Talk is your Ticket.

When you use your Power to Engage, you can Cash in your Ticket. When you master the Rules of Engagement, the world around you will pay attention and listen to you.

So I want to encourage you to develop this craft. Join Toastmasters International and sign up to speak regularly. Read books about presentation and communication skills. Watch videos of people delivering presentations, including TED Talkers, Toastmasters World Champions and finalists, motivational speakers, business leaders, political power-talkers, and professional speakers. Invest in every opportunity there is to learn about this craft and how to master it.

And whenever you speak, be it in front of an audience at a conference, among colleagues at a meeting, with friends at a social gathering, or face-to-face at an interview, remember this one thing: Spend more time preparing before you speak. The Rules of E.N.G.A.G.E.M.E.N.T. can be wrapped up in two words....and believe it or not, neither word is ENGAGE.

The words are PREPARE and INTEND.

If you want people to pay attention to you, spend more time preparing intentionally what you want to say and spend more time preparing intentionally how you want to say it. Preparation and Intention are the cornerstones of my message to you. And the words "with strategic intention" are especially important too. Every single Rule of Engagement is a rule that should be mastered and applied with strategic intention before the moment when you actually speak. That's how you get people to pay attention to you!

In closing, minutes after not winning the 2014 World Championship of Public Speaking, my heart sank and this feeling of disappointment overwhelmed my thoughts because I so badly wanted to disappear or at least escape without being seen. If I could have done so and just locked myself in my hotel room until my flight back to New York...I would have...and yet I am so glad that I did not do that.

That sinking feeling only lasted a moment because in one minute, I was reminded of why we speak. We don't speak to win a championship or a trophy or even some kind of a grand prize (that's only for people with a Voice, people who "Got Talent", or people who think they can dance. There's no reality show for speakers...at least not yet...hmmm). We don't speak for a prize. We speak for the chance. We speak for the chance to make a difference in at least one person's life, whether it be to make her think, make him laugh, or make that person better. And yes, every time we speak, we have the power to do any of those things, and possibly a whole lot more. That is what makes speaking in front of people, whether it be on stage, in an interview, or during a sale, so incredibly crucial to your own personal, professional, and financial development, and to the development of everyone within the sound of your voice.

Every one of us can talk, and yet so many people are afraid to speak. Many others are not confident in their ability to speak effectively. Some people just wish they could get better at it. Actually, most of us wish we could get better at it.

I did not win the World Championship of Public Speaking in 2014! But I am proud to say that in a pool of 30,000 participants, I advanced to the finals as one of the nine best speakers in the world. Eight months of dedication to speaking landed me among the elite. And while I did not feel so "elite" when my name was not announced as the winner, I felt victorious when one audience member found his way to the front of the 3,000-seat auditorium to share with me that my words "changed" him; they "changed" the way he looks at his life. I am incredibly thankful that he made the effort to share how I influenced him. As I proudly stepped into the hallway to a crowd of Toastmasters who just experienced the 2014 Toastmasters International Speech Contest in Kuala Lumpur, Malaysia, I realized that the key to creating an impact is not just through the words we speak, but through the way we deliver those words.

Yes, speaking in front of people can be a scary thing to do, but you can conquer the fear and you can conquer the floor. I encourage you to make the effort because you have something to share. And now that you know the rules, make it your habit to follow the rules, until you master the Rules of ENGAGEMENT...because when you do, others will become better than they were before...because of you. And that will be the reason why all of those people will pay more attention to you!

<u>Notes</u>

Works Cited

1. Sepulvado, John. "Obama's 'Overnight Success In 2004 Was A Year In The Making." OPB, 19, May 2016.
2. Wilson, Scott. "In Demand: Washington's Highest (and Lowest) Speaking Fees.", ABCNews, 14, July 2014.
3. Hafford, W.B. "The Value of Public Speaking to the Future Engineer." Ohio State Engineer, November 1924.
4. Collins, Phillip. The Art of Speeches and Presentations. May 2012.
5. SlideGenius. "Content or Delivery: Which Matters Most in a Presentation." September 2015.
6. Furnham, Adrian, Ph.D, "The Secrets of Eye Contact Revealed." Psychology Today, December 2014.
7. Kinsey Goman, Carol. "Fascinating Facts About Eye Contact." Forbes Magazine, August 2014.
8. Richards, Regina. "Making It Stick: Memorable Strategies to Enhance Learning." 2003.
9. Sukel, Kayt, "Basal Ganglia Contribute to Learning, but Also Certain Disorders." 23, January 2007.
10. Feloni, Richard. "Here's a breakdown of the speech that won the 2015 World Championship of Public Speaking." Business Insider, 11, September 2015.
11. SlideShare. "TED Talk Takeaways: 8 Ways to Hook Your Audience." 30, July 2014.
12. Murphy Paul, Annie. "Your Brain on Fiction: The Neuroscience of Your Brain on Fiction." New York Times, 17, March 2012.
13. Stevenson, Doug. "Storytelling and Brain Science: This Is Your Brain on Story." Association for Talent Development. 26, July 2016.
14. Iacoboni, Marco. Mirroring People: The Science of Empathy and How We Connect with Others. 23, June 2009.
15. Holmes, Lindsay. "6 Reasons Good Posture Can Make Your Whole Day Better." Huffington Post, 3, October 2014.
16. Dowling, Catherine. "Change How You Feel: Change How You Breathe." PsychCentral, 17, May 2016.

17. Matta, Christy. "3 Ways to Relax in the Face of Stress." PsychCentral, 3, September 2012.
18. BBC News. "The Problem with Powerpoint." 19, August 2009.
19. Markowitz, Eric. "5 Tips for a Great Powerpoint Presentation." Inc., 17, February 2011.
20. Hustad, Megan. "PowerPoint Abuse: How To Kick the Habit." Fortune Magazine, 12, June 2012.
21. Teten, David. "How to Add Powerful (And Legal) Images to your Presentation." Forbes, 15, August 2013.
22. Gallo, Carmine. "How Tony Robbins Gets in Peak State for Presentations." Forbes, 24, February 2012.
23. Gallo, Carmine. "Thomas Jefferson, Steve Jobs, and the Rule of 3." Forbes, 2, July 2012.
24. ISPO News. "90 Percent of All Purchasing Decisions Are Made Subconsciously." January 2015.
25. Bushak, Lecia. "How Curiosity Enhances the Brain And Stimulates The Reward System To Improve Learning And Memory." Medical Daily, 2, October 2014.
26. Deft Communications, "Be Aware of Your Time Limit", 21, April 2015.
27. Hofmann, George. "Our Fear of Silence." PsychCentral, 29, July 2017.
28. Sommerfeld, Julia. "Human Brain Gets a Kick Out of Surprises." MSNBC, 15, April.
29. Gallo, Carmine. "The One Habit That Brilliant TED Speakers Practice Up To 200 Times." Forbes, 17, March 2014.